ELECTION '45

Reflections on the Revolution in Britain

ELECTION '45

Reflections on the Revolution in Britain

Austin Mitchell

Fabian Society
Bellew Publishing · London

The author and the Fabian Society would like to thank the Webb Memorial Trust for their generous support, without which this book would not have been possible.

To Sykes

who inherits the
next half-century

This edition first published in Great Britain in 1995

Bellew Publishing Company Limited
8 Balham Hill, London SW12 9EA

ISBN 1 85725 109 1

Typeset in the UK by Antony Gray
Printed and bound by Hartnolls Ltd, Cornwall

Contents

Foreword
by the Rt Hon. Tony Blair MP
Leader of the Labour Party

The fiftieth anniversary of the 1945 election is an important occasion for the Labour Party and the country. Labour in 1945 combined idealism and practicality in equal measure to lead a national crusade for a Britain based on social justice, equality of opportunity and social solidarity. Out of the ruins of war, the 1945 Labour government set out to fulfil the age-old promise of a 'land fit for heroes'. To a remarkable extent, it succeeded

The Second World War was a people's war, fought in the name of democracy and humanity against fascism. Labour promised a people's peace. It delivered a national insurance system to provide security against unemployment and old age. It established a national, integrated rail system. It was instrumental in the establishment of international institutions – like the UN, born in London in 1948. And it set up the pride and joy of British socialism – the National Health Service. What is more, at the end of its period in office, the Labour government secured the largest vote ever achieved by the Party.

Election '45 is a remarkable political testament to a remarkable political era. In the words of the real-life actors of the time, it summons up the spirit of hope, expectation and – in the cases of defeated Tory candidates – bemusement that marked the 1945 General Election. The lesson of 1945 should be clear: democratic socialism can be both practical and popular.

A party that lives in the past is doomed to die. But a party that neglects the past is doomed to fail. Our job is to honour the past but look forward to the future. This book helps us to do both.

Tony Blair

NO MORE DOLE QUEUES . . . . SO IT'S
LABOUR
FOR SECURITY
VOTE LABOUR FOR SELF-RESPECTING JOBS
LABOUR X

Preface

This is the story of the 1945 election told by those who took part: Fabians, candidates and elected MPs of the three main parties. Of sixteen hundred and eighty-three candidates, a hundred and ten are still alive half a century later. Of six hundred and forty MPs, forty-three are still alive, half of them in the House of Lords. I was privileged to interview thirty-three, the most enjoyable piece of research I have ever done, and I am grateful to them all for bringing to life an election thoroughly embalmed at the time by Alison Readman and R. B. McCullum in the first Nuffield election study. Most of the material for the book was gathered in taped interviews and the essence of what people were saying is here transcribed and attributed to them under their 1945 titles. Some, mostly Fabians, sent written accounts, and I am also grateful to Tony Lambton for his vivid account of Chester-le-Street and to Stuart Ball for the unpublished extracts from Cuthbert Headlam's diary.

The resulting book is their collective effort, though it also embodies the hard work of a lot of other people. Stella Meldrum put the idea into my head. The Fabian Society Executive backed it and the society's 1945 Committee pushed it to fruition. Anne Reisinger researched and organised it, Matthew Seward assisted and Tim Grewal kept the office running while I burbled about the past, a habit of mine he is used to. Joyce Benton, Pat Murray and Lynn Watkin transcribed the interviews, typed up the text and coped with all the changes. I don't know how they stayed sane. Particularly since they also had to run a 1995 constituency whose MP had regressed fifty years. The work has been theirs, the pleasure and the privilege mine, any achievement that of the people who were so generous with their memories of Labour's annus mirabilis. May it be repeated soon!

Austin Mitchell, Grimsby

1945 RESULT

Younger, Major Kenneth (Labour) MP 1945–59)	28,484
Womersley, Sir Walter (Conservative) (MP 1924–45)	18,841
Labour majority (never equalled since)	9,643

26 July 1945

Grimsby celebrates the election of its first ever Labour MP, Major the Honourable Kenneth Younger, on leave from the Intelligence Corps, member of the Labour Party since 1937, selected for Grimsby in December 1944.

Younger noted in his diary: 'We ended up with 28,484, a majority of 9,643. That was of course much bigger than any of us had hoped. I was delighted but knew that I personally could claim only minor credit for it. For old Labour supporters who had been on the losing side so often (scarcely even daring to believe in victory), it was tremendously exhilarating.

CHAPTER ONE

The Road to Revolution

Britain has had three revolutions, the Civil War, the Glorious Revolution and 1945. The first two changed the élite and the regime. The 1945 election did that in a massive transfusion of new blood but also ushered in a new social, political and economic settlement. A radical programme was carried through by a government of giant figures who built a welfare state, and an economy run for full employment and high and sustainable growth on Keynesian lines with its commanding heights in public ownership. That settlement endured until Margaret Thatcher's counter-revolution.

1945 was radical but also conservative, building on the wartime ethos of collective sacrifice and total mobilisation for the common purpose. Labour's victory was unexpected but its measures well prepared, and the whole thing was very British in being carried through by insiders, not alienated outsiders overthrowing everything. Labour, the instrument of change, had been in government in coalition with the Conservatives ever since 1940, with Clement Attlee Deputy Prime Minister, and Herbert Morrison and Ernest Bevin running the home front. By 1945 the party had standing, authority and experience.

That wartime coalition rested on a political truce. The election due in 1940 had been postponed until after the war. The parties agreed not to contest by-elections and to suspend activity. Yet beneath the surface, and largely unknown because neither tested by polls nor boosted by media hype, the mood of the country was changing, most dramatically in the forces. There the auguries indicated a massive shift of opinion against an incumbent class and the leadership which had stumbled into war; Tories put this down to subversion by the Army Bureau of Current Affairs.

ABCA in action: the Army School of Education in Pachmarchi, India

✘ What was not readily appreciated until after the election was the effect many people believed the Army Bureau of Current Affairs had upon the soldiers' vote, because a large number of the people who were manning the ABCA, and who were responsible for the lectures on public affairs given to soldiers, were, in fact, left wing. I think I'm right in saying that the head of the Army Bureau of Current Affairs was Colonel Wigg.

Major LEONARD CAPLAN (Conservative, North Hammersmith)

✘ I never concealed my socialist beliefs in the army. In fact I invited my first CO back to my flat and he could see all the rows of my books, including the complete works of Lenin and the lot, I never concealed a thing, and I got promotion in spite of it, but I think not because of it.

King George VI was coming round to our regiment. So a security wallah turned up and said had I got any dubious characters in the unit, so I said that we had a couple of jewel robbers, Peter Martin Jenkins and another character. 'Oh,' he said, 'I don't mean those. Have you got any socialists?' I said, 'Yes I'm one,' and he looked a little aghast and said, 'Isn't that a little unusual,' and after that the conversation terminated. I told my CO and he roared his head off. But it showed you how the official mind worked in those days.

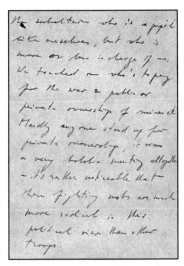

A letter home from a fighter pilot

To-day we've been having lectures on square bashing & square bashing & I suppose it'll be the same until Friday. We had a sort of ABCA meeting this afternoon under the subaltern who is a pupil like ourselves, but who is more or less in charge of us. We touched on who's to pay for the war & public or private ownership of mines etc. Hardly any one stood up for private ownership, it was a very bolshie meeting altogether – it's rather noticeable that these fighting mobs are much more radical in their political views than other troops.

When the ABCA came into the army I had been posted to a different unit. I was charged with a company of 600 people. My CO, who was probably the most reactionary Tory ever alive, was surprised with the zeal with which one of his company commanders insisted on personal responsibility for the supervision of the ABCA instruction. I was to take the entire company on a Thursday afternoon. I used it to explain how the British economy worked.

Major DONALD BRUCE (Labour, Portsmouth North)

✘ I'd been attached to the Education Corps in the army when Beveridge came out and I was conducting the Army Bureau of Current Affairs. We talked about Beveridge and I think the army vote went almost solidly in favour of the Labour Party because we advocated the implementation of Beveridge so far as the health service, national insurance, and the rest were concerned. The military vote was normally a patriotic vote but they'd had a basin full and they were determined we'd won the war and the only way to win the peace was to get a Labour government. So, I think people like me and Denis Healey, and others who were in uniform, did our bit in our own way, propaganda-wise, to make sure that the military vote went with Labour.

Lieutenant WILLIE HAMILTON (Labour, West Fife)

✘ Part of my job in the forces was to be a lecturer in current affairs in the ABCA, which involved trying to talk to the troops in as reasonably impartial a way as any Liberal could, and one got a very strong feeling from them that they were pretty disillusioned with the Conservative Party as a whole, and particularly with the days of appeasement and events before the war. The swing in that sense didn't surprise me but, of course, in my youthful naïvety I thought we might get it rather than the Labour Party.

Lieutenant BASIL WIGODER (Liberal, Bournemouth)

✘ The ABCA was meant to be a morale booster. That is why Montgomery backed it. We didn't think of it in those terms. We thought of it as trying to spread the word. Get soldiers to think about politics and if the subject was presented properly they would think sensibly about it. Vote Labour because it was in their interests.

PETER KINGSFORD

What Tories saw as a plot could hardly have subverted the entire soldiery had not the experience of war and the determination not to return to the thirties all pointed in the same direction. Forces and civilians learned the lesson of war: total mobilisation for a common purpose could achieve it.

At home the Gallup Poll had been charting voting intentions quarterly since before the war. Its 1945 polls put Labour well ahead but were largely ignored.

POLLS IN 1945				
Voting Intention	Conservative	Labour	Liberal	Other
February 1945	27.5	47.5	12.5	12.5
April 1945	28.0	47.0	14.0	11.0
June 1945	32.0	45.0	15.0	8.0

The polls were neither understood nor trusted and their lesson was not rammed home and amplified. Even Gallup lacked confidence and failed to predict a Labour victory. Media and government, focused on the war, missed the trend. Others detected the swell but assumed that it was a wartime aberration. So the shift broke surface only at by-elections where Common Wealth challenged in Tory constituencies.

✘ Common Wealth was started by Sir Richard Acland in order to break the electoral truce. It put up candidates and made sure there was an election. They were essentially a ginger group and not intended to have a long-term future. They existed solely for breaking the electoral truce. The idea of Common Wealth was that the members were interested in the common wealth. It was essentially a Socialist party but not a radical Socialist party. You had to have a policy not just an election-fighting machine. Its policy was a bit woolly but its electoral tactics were good, its canvassing activities were tuned to a fine art. I remember one occasion when we were being instructed on how to conduct a canvass; the idea was that five or six people should go into one row of houses, rather than one person into each row. Five of us would knock at five doors simultaneously and when the householder came out we would start a discussion between the five householders and five canvassers in the street. I think it was a good idea. The Common Wealth party was to the right of Labour and the left of Liberals.

TOM MELDRUM (Watford Fabian)

✘ My sympathies were 'left' but I had never joined the Labour Party because I did not like its domination in its internal voting processes by the trade unions and not by its members. I had joined Sir Richard Acland's Common Wealth and a branch was started in Harpenden with several members.

When the election came the Common Wealth did not contest any constituency within easy reach, so I offered my services to the local Labour organisation. Few of the local Labour supporters knew anything about election procedures. I took my part in leafleting, canvassing and election-day organisation and a few months later I came to realise that the only way to take part in left politics was through the Labour Party, in spite of my dislike of its domination by the trade unions (although I was a member of a union). I joined the party in Autumn 1945 and have been a member ever since.

JACK VINCENT (Bristol Fabian)

Common Wealth became both a skirmishing party and a recruiting contingent for Labour. By the end of the war it had won four seats from the Tories. Its second successful candidate, Hugh Lawson, told us:

✘ I was thirty-one when I won the Skipton by-election of January 1944 and became the youngest member of the House of Commons.

In the House I was very active in raising matters concerning those in the armed services and in particular their political rights and I got many letters from them. In the army I'd been very active in political education, through the ABCA and other means. So even if what I did in the three weeks of the 1945 General Election campaign had little political significance, what I had done for political awareness among servicemen and women in the previous eighteen months was of great importance, for, more than anything else, it was the flood tide of the service vote (and of their friends and kin at home) that overwhelmed Churchill and swept Labour to power.

In 1944 I was a soldier recently returned from long service overseas, I was a middle-class professional engineer and a university graduate. The unsuccessful Conservative graduate was an elderly mill-owner and farmer. I believe that it was from the date of my election that the Labour Party began to look for candidates to fight the post-war election who were of my type so that indirectly my success helped to produce the talented 1945 Parliamentary Party.

HUGH LAWSON (elected Skipton January 1944,
defeated as Common Wealth candidate Harrow West 1945)

In West Derbyshire an independent Labour man defeated the then Duke of Devonshire's eldest son, making the Duke one of the first to see what was happening.

✘ My father had been MP for West Derbyshire from 1924 to 1938 and I regret to say he had come to treat it rather as a rotten borough because when my grandfather died and he succeeded he put in his brother-in-law. He then went off to the Middle East in the war and the seat became vacant and my father arranged for my brother to be the Tory candidate.

This was a mistake. It was, I believe, a very bitter by-election. I was away in Italy but it was very bitter. The Labour candidate was a man called Charlie White who was a political enemy of my father's. Anyway my brother was well and truly beaten by five thousand votes. He then went off to war and was killed, and in 1945 Charlie White just held it by a hundred and fifty votes. I understand my father, as a result of this, foresaw a Labour victory because he realised the trend was going Labour's way. I'm not sure he didn't make a bit of money on bets on it too.

Lord ANDREW CAVENDISH (Conservative, Chesterfield)

Activists were more in touch, but few in number. The Tories had mothballed their organisation and, for once, felt a sulky sense of disadvantage. Cuthbert Headlam, former Tory MP who hoped to get back in 1945, worried that:

✘ Elections cannot be won without organisation – and our organisation has been in cold storage for too long while the left-wing people have been busy all the time . . . if we had waited until October for the election, the Labour people would have been no stronger than they are today and we should have been able to get our organisation going again.

Parliament and Politics in the Age of Churchill and Attlee: The Headlam Diaries 1935–51, Stuart Ball (ed.), to be published in 1996

✘ The last conference the Tory Party had had after war had been declared was in Liverpool. The first item on the agenda, the Director General, chap named Topping, says, 'We disband our Conservative organisation. We concentrate the whole of our efforts on winning the war. Nothing must come in the way. Not even loyalty to party.' I was very unpopular because I got up and said, 'You're doing the wrong thing on this.'

The Tory Party agents were usually the colonels and the people on the reserve lists, ex-this, that and the other, of the First World War. I said, 'The minute you do that you're disbanding our machine, but the Labour Party won't. And the Unions, they won't cut themselves out. So you'll be leaving intact all of the paraphernalia of getting over their party's points of view when we've disbanded our alternative. You mustn't do that.' And I was looked upon as somebody that was being unpatriotic, not facing up to things. But I'd been fighting elections and had a feeling. And that is what happened.

Lieutenant HARMAR-NICHOLLS (Conservative, Nelson & Colne)

Labour's structures remained intact, the unions were political as well as industrial machines, and Fabians and other activists were organised and ready.

✘ An awful lot of people were Fabians. In fact local societies made an enormous contribution to Labour's success. Many of the candidates were local society secretaries or treasurers. We were all

Fabians and active in local societies or socialist propaganda committees. Local societies were what really kept political activity going during the war and what kept people aware. Victor Gollancz's effort with the Left Book Club and summer schools and socialist propaganda really made an enormous contribution. I have always felt the Fabian Society has underestimated the contribution that won the General Election. It made all the difference because there was so much of a sort of embryo organisation, and the people who appeared were local society officers and familiar with organising.

DOROTHY FOX (Meopham Fabian)

✘ During the war you couldn't be active in the Labour Party because there was a complete truce. We joined the Common Wealth party with Dick Acland because we needed some activity, and people around us, like Sybil Wingate and so on, were all in Common Wealth to have some political activity and prepare for the election. So we then used through Sybil Wingate a lot of those people in the 1945 election.

IRENE WAGNER (London Fabian)

✘ Parties had been mothballed officially – but there were parties everywhere, and they were gaining strength. We had a very active party in Barkstone Ash. We continued to recruit. You could officially disband, but nobody ever received any instruction to disband. In fact there were suggestions that you might consider carrying on because there was a point of view to be put forward whether there was an election or not, and you couldn't put it forward unless you'd got some semblance of an organisation. So I think the fact that we had sixty-two official delegates at the selection conference indicated that there was some strength of membership. The region was set up in 1941 and I was one of those responsible and obviously it wasn't going to just be an organisation that sat down and did nowt. It was going to prepare for the future. With the obvious intention that there would be elections in due course. So it was a very active party. We had a full-time secretary and a full-time women's organiser, Sarah Barker, and Len Williams was the secretary.

We had strong organisations throughout the mining areas, not politically, but industrially, and industrially of course they did the political job too. The Party was taking a line that once the war was over the need for coalition should come to an end. Though some of our national people were a little reluctant. Some of the leaders added a cautionary note not to rush things too much. Better to have a full electoral register than one that was considerably out of date. It might be better to exert more influence with the National Government for a bit than to rush into something, because Churchill was a very popular man and would be very difficult to beat.

BERT HAZELL (Labour, Barkston Ash)

For a brief moment of opportunity Labour was readier, stronger and better able to paddle with the tide. Yet Labour ministers seemed unaware of the opportunity and the Coalition broke up for accidental rather than opportunistic reasons. It was to end with the war. In Europe that finished on 7 May, with an unconditional surrender announced on 8 May. When Churchill proposed to carry the Coalition on to the end of the war against Japan, Labour ministers were not averse to the idea but were pulled into line by the National Executive and the Party Conference. Even then they preferred an autumn poll and a new register. It was Churchill who decided to go immediately to capitalise on gratitude to the leadership which had won the war.

Thus the 1945 story begins with Labour's conference in Blackpool ending the Coalition, endorsing the manifesto 'Let Us Face the Future' and precipitating the General Election.

✘ I went as a candidate to the Labour Party Conference in May of 1945 and there was quite a strong current of feeling that we ought not to rush a General Election. But on the other hand, the rank and file of the movement made it perfectly clear that the time had come for an early General Election, and the sooner the better. And there was an air of excitement that I'd never witnessed before or witnessed since. There was an air of expectancy that you could feel as you entered the conference on Whit Monday morning. I don't know, it may have been something personal in the fact that I'd been adopted as a candidate and knew I'd be in the thick of it, that might have had some influence on my experience – but I thought, as we entered the conference hall, it was a tide of tremendous excitement, very difficult to explain, but it was there. And the Chair in that year was Ellen Wilkinson, who, herself, gave a tremendously inspiring start to the conference. There was a huge fear that if we didn't have a Labour government we'd have the mass unemployment that followed the 1918 victory. We didn't want to see that happen again. The rank and file of the party literally pushed the leadership. When Churchill gave his ultimatum there was not exactly a revolt at the conference but it was obvious when decisions were taken by the size of the majority. It wasn't open revolt, there weren't a lot of personalities. It was a declared intention that we were going to have an election, and the leadership were wise enough to recognise that they couldn't do much about it. It was overwhelming.

The *Daily Herald* was first on the scene. They issued an invitation to every prospective parliamentary candidate to take their photograph free of charge, because there would be very little time for that when the election was called. I never even had a chance to change because everybody just queued up, so I'd just got an ordinary sports jacket on. The photo was taken inside the conference hall by the *Daily Herald*, and I used it for the 1950 election as well as 1945.

BERT HAZELL (Labour, Barkston Ash)

✘ I went to the rather memorable Labour Party Conference at Blackpool at the end of May, and everyone knew when the election was going to be by then. I rather think of the campaign as beginning at that Blackpool conference. It was a great electioneering jamboree and I certainly remember a lot of speeches. I remember Bevin's speech: 'If we have too much butter I'd put a second pat of butter on everybody's plate in the works' canteen.' I remember a speech of Hugh Dalton's which rang with every sort of oratorical cliché and ended, 'And when the last trumpet sounds we shall be there battling up the hill . . . ' or whatever it was. I remember a rather good speech of Major Denis Healey's. He was in battledress. I was only a captain but I was in service dress for some reason or other. Denis had his cuffs turned back which gave him a very sort of macho appearance and he'd just come back from Italy and denounced the ruling classes of Europe as being corrupt. A lot of dreadful things, but a striking speech. Cripps had been expelled from the Labour Party at the Southport conference of 1939. He was given a great reception, speaking from the floor, when he said ,'I am bound to say I much prefer the climate of Blackpool to that of Southport.' So you see quite vivid memories remain in one's mind.

Captain ROY JENKINS (Labour, Solihull)

Then & Now – but still a sports jacket   May 1945 – the left leads the way

✘ I was sent back to England just in time to go to the party conference which was a wonderful experience because we were very idealistic. I made a very left-wing speech about the importance of the Labour Party, when it won power, not being like the man who carried the Red Flag in front of the motor car of capitalism. I met a lot of people who had been friends, like Roy Jenkins who was standing in that election, and people I hadn't met before, like John Freeman who had been serving in northern Europe as a brigade major; we remained friends after the war. There is a picture of me in *Picture Post*.

The atmosphere was 'get up and go' and everybody was left wing. Everybody wanted to work with the Russians in peace as in war. Ernie Bevin made a great speech in which he said 'left can talk to left' meaning the Soviet Union. But the key thing was we wanted to rebuild a decent society based on social justice. This was the theme really of practically every serving man who spoke at the conference.

Major DENIS HEALEY (Labour, Pudsey and Otley)

✘ I felt the election had been called as conference drew to a close, when Ellen Wilkinson urged everybody to go back to their constituency ready to fight. It was obvious as soon as ever the leaders got back to London they would be telling Winston Churchill that the Party would want to fight straight away. So I well recall telephoning my agent and asking him to book rooms for an eve-of-the-poll meeting. We had a pretty shrewd idea when it was going to happen and we took a gamble, because otherwise everybody else would want the rooms. So we literally started our campaign there. Immediately we got back from the conference we started fixing up the meetings.

BERT HAZELL (Labour, Barkston Ash)

✖ I remember that on the day that Parliament was actually dissolved I went into the Tea Room and found myself sitting alone with Mr Attlee and I asked him how he thought the result would go. He said to me he thought it would go well but he didn't expect to win the election though he thought they would take a lot of seats away from us; he didn't see the people turning out Churchill at that stage. Those words I remember so very clearly.

ROBERT GRANT-FERRIS (Conservative, St Pancras North)

WHAT'S THE HURRY?

CHAPTER TWO

Scramble

1945 was the last election where the weight of activity and excitement was more local than national. Politics, in cold storage for five years, had not yet become habit or spectator sport. No media circus had yet developed to whip up excitement. War was still on as the weight of the war effort shifted against Japan – a war expected at that stage to last another two years. Five million men and women were in the forces, most of them scattered around the world.

So the election was an unexpected but hectic holiday. The timetable was compressed: announcement on 23 May when the Coalition ended, dissolution on 15 June, nominations by 25 June, then a short campaign up to polling day on 5 July. New men and a few new women began to come forward from all over the world.

✘ I was selected in 1943 and I went away the very same night to join a convoy in Liverpool and I didn't get back to the constituency until the campaign was well on its way in 1945, because when the election was called I was serving in the Indian Ocean on my way to Australia to join the British Pacific Fleet. The Admiralty said you can come home to fight the election but they didn't provide any means of transport. So I got back to Ceylon and after a few days I hitched a ride in an aircraft to Karachi where I languished fretting all the time because the campaign was starting. Then I got a lift in an American aircraft to Andrews Airfield just south of Cairo and from that we got to London where I arrived home to the astonishment of my wife who had been expecting me but had had no news. There were my two small daughters, both of whom had got measles. So Audrey was torn between looking after the children and trying to keep me out of the way of the measles in case I couldn't even get to the constituency.

Lieutenant JAMES CALLAGHAN (Labour, Cardiff South)

✗ By an extraordinary chapter of accidents I decided during the war that I really wanted to go into politics somehow to stop the next war. To my amazement two constituencies wrote to me. One was Penrith which was a dead safe Tory seat, I think held from the war onwards by Willie Whitelaw until he came to the home of the living dead. The other was Pudsey and Otley which was shaped like the letter H because it was a constituency formed of the fragments of other constituencies which fell out on redistribution. I took that one to try for.

I was in Italy at the time in the army and so I wrote a speech to be given to the selection conference. It was given by a friend of my father's, who didn't really know me at all and it is quite an interesting speech in a way; I kept a copy of it because it is very much the way we all felt in the army at that time. I said that I'm only one of hundreds of young men now in the forces who long for the opportunity to realise their political ideals by actively fighting an election for the Labour Party. These men in their turn represent millions of soldiers, sailors and airmen who want socialism and have been fighting magnificently to save a world in which socialism is possible. Then I made a great appeal for making the war worthwhile and the suffering everybody had endured, including non-combatants in Italy where I had been serving. I said only a more glorious future can make up for this annihilation of the past. I think for most of us of that generation idealism was the overwhelming force which drove us into politics, although we hadn't a clue really precisely what we wanted. I was incredibly ignorant. I remember during the campaign itself I was asked a question about exports and I said I thought it was criminal to be exporting shoes to people in Australia when there were kids in Barnsley who had no shoes at all.

The extraordinary thing in a way is that for the wartime generation economics scarcely existed. It was all about ideals and building a better world. We were very conscious of the domestic problems in Britain, having lived through the slump, but we were totally unconscious of the sort of economic problems the post-war Labour government would face when we won.

Major DENIS HEALEY (Labour, Pudsey and Otley)

✗ When the question of the election came up, which was of course immediately, May the 8th, I applied to get on the 'B' list and, to my surprise, they put me on it. Subsequently I thought they must have considered it a hopeless seat otherwise they might not

Our cook's been called up – he's a parliamentary candidate for Much Nattering

have done so, because before the war I was fairly active in Paddington as convenor of the local Left Book Club.

They sent me a list of the constituencies who were looking, so I put up for Portsmouth. I must say that I didn't look at the majority otherwise I would have been deterred because it was a naval seat, formerly occupied by Admiral Sir Roger Keyes, and after that by Bubbles James – so generally speaking, I should think that head office's scepticism about my chances was fully justified. It didn't occur to me, incidentally, that I might lose. I was one of those who, during the war, thought, and had good reason to feel by the reaction of my own troops, that a sea change was going to happen. So it wasn't altogether unexpected that we ultimately won.

I was in Reims at the time, and I came back to Portsmouth and, in spite of being a 'brown job' complete with Sam Browne and the lot, I was adopted. Then the General Election was declared and I returned for the campaign. It was a most exhilarating campaign. It really was absolutely wonderful.

Major DONALD BRUCE (Labour, Portsmouth North)

✗ I had a sort of settled disposition, partly hereditary but partly on interest, that I wanted to be a Member of Parliament. My father was a Member of Parliament, and I was very politically – I now think looking back, almost over-politically – active at Oxford. As the war began to move towards its end, I was in the army and, like a lot of people, began to think about a parliamentary seat. Therefore over the autumn, winter, spring of 1944/5 I went to a lot of selection conferences which shows that I wasn't selected at the first one by any means. I have a really strong experience of selection conferences. I missed one by one vote, the Sparkbrook division of Birmingham, others by more votes. Mind you one was beaten by an interesting selection of people. Woodrow Wyatt beat me for Aston, fairly closely. It wasn't all that easy and when I was selected for Solihull, which God knows was no plumb of a Labour seat by any stretch of the imagination, I beat Eddie Shackleton by one vote. So eventually, pretty late on for a July election, I was adopted for the Solihull division of Warwickshire which of course was almost entirely Birmingham suburban division, one of the most solidly Conservative seats in the country. Indeed it remained solid against my onslaughts in 1945.

Captain ROY JENKINS (Labour, Solihull)

✗ I was on my way to India, having left Normandy, so while I was in England, briefly, I went to the selection conference at Aston in Birmingham, where they had a huge Tory majority. I turned up there and I was pretty inarticulate. But that didn't seem to matter very much, because what I had done was stay with the agent in Aston, in one of those back-to-back houses. Roy Jenkins had gone to stay in a hotel so he was thought to be rather standoffish in not wishing to stay with one of the leading lights of the local party. But it gave me an advantage I suppose – only time I've had an advantage over Roy in my life. So I was selected and he wasn't. Then I went to India with the full knowledge that when the war ended I'd fight the seat, though I never expected to win it.

Major WOODROW WYATT (Labour, Birmingham, Aston)

✗ I was Deputy Regional Comissioner for South East England. The country was divided into twelve regions and the Regional Commissioner was an almighty man and Hartley Shawcross and myself were his deputies. We had all the services, air-raid precautions, fire brigade, fire watching. We had to run the whole region in the expectation that some day we might do it in reality if there was an invasion.

When I was DRC the Rochester and Chatham party said they wanted a candidate and would I be it. I was seeking to come into Parliament and I said Yes. So they nominated me and it was then raised in the House of Commons with Herbert Morrison that a civil servant had no right to be a parliamentary candidate. Morrison was able to reply that I wasn't a civil servant, I was a DRC and if I wanted to be a parliamentary candidate, I could be. So I became the candidate for Rochester and Chatham.

ARTHUR BOTTOMLEY (Labour, Rochester and Chatham)

✗ My father and grandfather were Liberals so I was born a Liberal, I was president of the Liberal Club at Oxford and then in 1932, when we had vast unemployment far bigger than we've ever had since, three and a quarter million in a much smaller population and it was due largely to the dumping of foreign goods, I thought that the Conservatives who wanted imperial preference and some protection had the right ideas and that the Liberals were wrong to stick to free trade. So I became a National Liberal and of course we naturally became allies of the Conservatives but remained for years an independent party. We had a rather small organisation over in Bridge Street.

I'd been in the army throughout the war and I'd been overseas in the desert and in Libya and Egypt. If you could be chosen as a candidate for interview you were home for a week, if you were chosen to fight the election even if you didn't win you were home for a month and if you won you were home for the last three years of the war – and I'd been terribly ill and I wanted to get home. Normally I would have waited until I'd revived my practice and been made a King's Counsel but on this occasion I thought 'well all right, it's not only a way of getting home, it's a way of getting into politics before it's too late'. So that's why I was lucky to be chosen for Huntingdonshire.

When I went down for interview I found that they'd already chosen one National Liberal candidate who said to himself, 'I'm too old' – he was in late middle age – 'for this huge constituency, three hundred and sixty-five square miles, eighty villages and five towns, and I'm not going to stand.' He said this to them only four weeks before polling day. So they arranged for me to go down there and they arranged for a wing commander in the Royal Air

Blackburn selects Barbara

Force to go too. We were the only two but I obviously knew more about politics than he did and for some reason best known to themselves they chose me.

Major DAVID RENTON (National Liberal, Huntingdonshire)

✘ It was the first example of positive discrimination and it was so successful I've been in favour of it ever since, because the trouble for women is not being given an opportunity to show what they can do. Various people approached me in constituencies. The first one was Crewe where men absolutely refused to have a woman on the short-list. But then Blackburn Labour Party approached me, the women's section, because the selection committee which was all men had got an all-male short-list of six white male trade unionists. The women's section went on strike and they said we are not going to make any more cups of tea or address any more envelopes unless there is a woman on the short-list. Terrified at the thought of having to make their own tea, the men gave in.

The interesting thing is the women didn't say 'we want Barbara Castle because she's got a future' or 'she's bright' or something. They said, 'We want the principle that there should be a woman on the short-list.' Having won that point they then went to Francis Kirby who was the women's regional organiser for the north-west and said give us the name of a good woman. Well, she said, there is that young Barbara Betts – because I wasn't married then – who made a speech at Party Conference. All right, they said, we'll nominate her, and they'd never even met me.

Even then I wouldn't have got the seat, because, of course, the predominantly male selection committee just assumed if you'd got a good man you didn't put a woman in over him. But also they wanted the trade union sponsorship. They wanted the money. We happened to be in a double-member constituency, so they had two votes. They cast the first one for a white male trade unionist to bring them some money and then the second one they said, well, its a bonus. Why not go for that rather fiery young redhead? So I was selected with John Edwards, a very nice and very able young man. The men said women won't vote for women, which is one of those comforting myths that men cocoon themselves in. So it was women there who voted for a woman. It was predominantly a textile area when I first went there and of course there are a lot of women in the textile industries. They were so loyal. They were so excited to have a woman to fight their battles for them.

BARBARA CASTLE (Labour, Blackburn)

✘ I was rather on the left of the Liberal Party. I believed in the social reform programme which they undertook in the 1906–14 government and I had been very impressed with that. Everybody thought in 1945 that there was going to be a rebirth. We all felt that this was an opportunity to stake a claim. I felt very strongly that it was important that there should be a strong Liberal element in the politics of the country. I came back from South East Asia.

I was a wing commander so I was given permission to come back and fight it, and Bernard Braine, who was a Conservative, and Willie Ross, an officer in South East Asia Command, and I all came back together and cancelled each other out. Mountbatten said, 'You can go back. I don't mind you going back provided you lose.' I said, 'I think I shall probably do so.' So he was right.

Wing Commander ALAN CAMPBELL-JOHNSON
(Liberal Salisbury and South Wilts)

✘ I decided whilst I was on leave that I wanted to be in the election because it was obvious to me that it was going to be the first time that there would be an independent Labour majority. So I popped in on Reg Wallis, the regional organiser. I told him that we were going to win the next election and I'd like to take part in it. So he said, 'Well you can't get a decent seat now,' so I said, 'I don't care if it's not a decent seat, I don't want to win it, I just want to be a part of it.' He said the only one in Manchester that was free was a hopeless seat called the Exchange Division. I said, 'That'll do me,' and he replied that he could get me a seat in Liverpool with a better chance. I said the Exchange would do for me.

So they put me on the short-list, and then I got a telephone call from one of the executive to tell me that there was no point in my turning up for the selection process because the executive had already decided that it was in favour of a man called Austin, a furniture manufacturer, Austin Suites. He had told them that he would put money into the constituency. I asked my wife to go to the pictures. But she said, 'No, your duty is to turn up; whether they do their duty, that's a different matter.' So I went.

You must realise that in those days because of the war there was no party left. The total number of members in the party in the Exchange when I was elected was some thirty odd, so there were no delegates or anything from ward parties. The executive amounted to eleven people. They were in favour of Austin, so I was told. Still, I made my speech, and all he got was ten out of the eleven executive votes. I got the rest of the votes and I was nominated. To his astonishment, and to mine.

Flying Officer HAROLD LEVER (Labour, Manchester Exchange)

✘ I have got politics in my blood, both my father's family and my mother's family were very high Tory and so I was anxious to stand. Also, it got me out of the army for the campaign which was the additional advantage. I tried the East End London seats, tried Dennis Skinner's seat in North East Derbyshire but luckily there was a chap on the North East Derbyshire selection committee who said they were looking for a candidate for Chesterfield. One of the great bits of good luck of my life because although I got well and truly beaten, I did actually reduce the Labour majority, which not so many many people did in 1945 and I made a lot of friends.

Lord ANDREW CAVENDISH (Conservative, Chesterfield)

✘ Somewhere round about 1938 I was being favourably considered for a number of possible seats when it was suggested to me that I might put myself forward for the constituency of North Hammersmith. I did not consider it a sufficiently good seat for what I regarded as my talents but I was persuaded to put my name forward for the next General Election, which was bound to take place not later than 1940, because if I did not win the seat I was still sufficiently young to put myself forward for better seats.

At that time, having been called to the Bar in 1935, I was doing reasonably well, and I did not find the financial request – and it was no more than a request – that was made to me for financial assistance unbearable; I cannot now remember how much I pledged but I think it may have been in the order of £100 or £200 per year as my subscription to the local association. So I was adopted. But the best-laid schemes of mice and men 'gang aft agley'. The war came along and there was no election in 1940. Instead I found myself in the armed forces.

At the time the war ended I was in fact recovering in a convalescent home just above Darjeeling but being at that time an adopted parliamentary candidate I was, like all such who were serving overseas, immediately recalled to England. I was unfit to travel by air, so I did three days' travel by train to Bombay and there caught a boat from Bombay going to England. If my recollection is right the boat left Bombay on 17 May 1945. This boat was then proceeding north through the Red Sea when the news came over the wireless that the date for the General Election had been fixed. The boat that I was on was a slow boat and in those circumstances was unlikely to arrive in England in time for me to be formally adopted as a Conservative candidate. I therefore, without benefit of movement orders, got myself off the boat at Alexandria, travelled by train to Cairo and, again without benefit of movement orders, managed to hop aboard an RAF plane which brought me to England at the beginning of June. Just in time to be adopted.

Major LEONARD CAPLAN
(Conservative, North Hammersmith)

✘ I got a scholarship through the NCLC to go to a summer school in Bangor in North Wales where I met some Fife miners. We immediately formed friendships, and they corresponded with me and sent me food parcels. I joined the army after a while but come 1945 they couldn't find a candidate to fight Willie Gallagher, who was then the sitting Communist MP for West Fife; he'd been there since 1935, and they thought it was hopeless to try and get this popular man out. They tried all kinds of folks in Fife. So scraping the barrel they found me at the bottom and they wrote to me and said would you like to be our candidate, Willie Hamilton, at the General Election? I was then in the army and hating every minute and the prospect of getting six weeks out of the army, three weeks for the campaign and three weeks to bring the votes in from all over the world, I thought that's great, even without pay. So I immediately said, yes, thank you very much. And that was how I got to West Fife. When I got there I didn't have any money, nor did the party. I didn't have any digs, and so I put this to them, I said where are you going to get the money from, where am I going to stay? 'Oh,' one of the miners in one of the villages said, 'We'll put you up Willie.' So I went up and was put up in a front room in a miner's home and we set about the thing.

Lieutenant WILLIE HAMILTON (Labour, West Fife)

✘ I expected to win when I came back from the war because I was fetched back in a hurry in order to have a nice seat and when I went up to Blackpool they said, 'You're a bit late, the Liberal will win, he is doing much better.' He was wise enough to be the captain of a cruiser called *Blackpool* so he was doing very well. Then I looked around and I found great enthusiasm.

The campaign was quite different from any other because it was old fashioned and you had great meetings – four hundred in the hall and fifteen hundred people on the pier. I'd been in the army for five years, I hadn't a clue about the main sort of political disputes other than what I had read in the newspapers. I had done a little bit of briefing myself and I just remembered what I felt before the war, when I was a sort of pro-Anthony Eden and pro-Winston man, and I wanted to become a Member of Parliament because I wanted to stop the unemployment. It was different from what I had been doing for five years. I had been doing things. People did what you asked them to do and we didn't have many arguments. But this was fun meeting people again, because one hadn't met lots of people, except for soldiers, I hadn't been in England for four years. I found addressing meetings difficult to begin with but eventually I was greatly helped by the hecklers – and Lancastrians are very good hecklers.

Brigadier A. R. W. LOW (Conservative, Blackpool North)

✘ First of all I must tell you that I had known Winston Churchill personally from the days when I was in the Oxford Union, when he came to speak there. I met him then and afterwards, being active in Conservative circles, I met him from time to time. In 1945 I was still on active service for the Royal Navy and one day I was sitting in the Admiralty and suddenly got a message to say, 'Report to 10 Downing Street at once.' I thought, my God, what have I done now? Anyway I went over to 10 Downing Street and when I was on the doorstep there was another commander, namely Peter Scott, and he said he'd been summoned in a similar fashion. We were ushered inside by Brigadier Harvie-Watt, who was the PA to Winston. He said, 'The old man wants to see you.' So we were ushered into the presence of the All Highest who said to us, 'Gentlemen, there is going to be a General Election and I want to tell you, gentlemen, that I have every constituency filled with support for me except two and I want you gentlemen to take them over.' That was that. We had to decide there and then. I chose Harrow East because I thought that Harrow sounded as if we had a better chance than anywhere else and Peter Scott took Wembley North. In the result, of course, we were both defeated but that's by the way. So then I was given leave from the navy and my first difficulty was to find a civvy suit.

Commander F. ASHE LINCOLN (Conservative, Harrow East)

✖ I was in the Fleet Air Arm and I'd fought along with A. J. Owen. I had gone to help him during the 1935 by-election and I desperately wanted to become MP for Aberdeen and Kincardineshire. I had fallen in love with the place and wrote to the local constituency association. The chairman was J. C. Forbes, a blacksmith in Glassel, a remote village miles from anywhere. In my pilot's uniform I travelled to Aberdeen and I took a bus and went to see Forbes who was still in his blacksmith's apron. He was a wonderful man. Blacksmiths and fishermen are the salt of the earth and I think he rather liked the cut of this youngster of twenty-three or twenty-four arriving in pilot's uniform and saying, 'Please, I want to be a candidate.' A couple of months later I was called up to a meeting in Aberdeen and selected and that was it. Forbes was one of the greatest men in my life. It is always the simple men who are the great upholders of democracy and decency.

Lieutenant JOHN JUNOR (Liberal, Kincardine and West Aberdeen)

✖ I thought I'd have a go because all of us at the end of the war felt that we had to do something about the country we were fighting for. My wife had been in Parliament during the war, and so I had a sort of political background, but whereas she inherited a Tory seat I stood as a Liberal because that was the prevailing feeling in the forces. It wasn't anti Conservative but it was pro left, I mean pro the future.

I'm not quite sure how it happened but the constituency next to old Percy Harris, who was a great Liberal figure in the pre-war House of Commons in Bethnal Green, was vacant from the Liberal point of view and somebody asked me if I'd stand. I went down and met them and that was that. It was very haphazard, nothing like the kind of procedures that go on today. I suppose I got adopted; I'm very vague on the dates here because you see I was in Germany when all this happened. I came home immediately after the Armistice but I'm not sure whether I'd been adopted before that or not. I think probably not. It all happened very quickly.

Of course I was an absolute babe in the wood politically, I had no real experience or indeed knowledge. My only appeal to those marvellous people in the East End was that I was a soldier and was going to look after their chaps who were coming back and try to make something of our country in peacetime. It was strong on emotion and not very strong on facts.

Major PAUL WRIGHT (Liberal, North East Bethnal Green)

✘ I was on the head office list because I wanted to become a Member of Parliament. I thought I might make the grade because I was invited to lunch by a Tory MP and I came out and said to myself, 'If a bloody fool like you can be an MP so can I.'

I attended a selection conference at Blackley and was fortunately selected – much to my surprise because it was obviously a hopeful seat at that time. There were very good people in for the selection, including the son of the local agent. I put the main cause of my being selected down to the fact that I am a Jew, because, in that part of Manchester we had the highest proportion of Catholics in any constituency and there was friction within the party between the substantial Catholic minority and the rest. One of the first questions I got after my opening remarks was directed towards my views on the freedom of religion. I said I was a Jew and, therefore, as a member of a minority, was very anxious that every minority should have the right to pursue the observance of its religious practices completely. This answer went down well and that, I assume, is the reason why they chose me.

JACK DIAMOND (Labour, Manchester, Blackley)

✘ My war record had been slightly unconventional. After ten months in the army I was invalided out of Sandhurst. I was always interested in politics and was anxious to fight a bad seat. There was no procedure to go through in those days. All my father did was to write to the President of the Northern Area, Lord Londonderry. He put me in touch with the Chairman. Sir Cuthbert Headlam MP, a sad, bitter, clever old man. I went to lunch with him and it was suggested I should stand for Chester-le-Street, my home constituency. Next I went to London to see Sir Harold Mitchell MP, the pale, obese, shifty, Vice-President of the Conservative Party. He received me with a greasy smile, shuffled papers on his desk, tried to put on an interested face, asked me if I had fought a seat in the last General Election. I said I was thirteen in 1935. That shut him up.

The Conservative member for nearby Stockton was Harold Macmillan, and his son Maurice went through the same process and became the Conservative candidate for nearby Seaham. He and his wife Katie were friends. Unlike myself, both came from political families and as children had helped their fathers during elections. Our selections may sound old fashioned but Central Office had great difficulty in finding Conservatives to fight in hopelessly Labour seats in Durham; both our constituencies had been Labour strongholds for fifty years. Also we said we would pay our election expenses. A popular gesture. The Conservative Party was broke at the time and local party leaders did not enjoy contributing to a lost cause.

Viscount LAMBTON (Conservative, Chester-Le-Street)

✘ I was in the Air Force and home on leave, and when I was walking through Holyhead, two or three councillors stopped me. I'd joined the Labour Party before the war, in 1938, and these old chaps were trade unionists and deacons of their chapels, and respected public men. They stopped me and said we're looking for a Labour candidate, what about it? I said that's a bit of a shock, I've got to go back to the Air Force in a couple of days, you know. Well, they said, we want you to think about it seriously.

They pressed me hard, and they knew me well. There was another problem, namely that my father was an active Liberal. He was a Presbyterian minister and an active Liberal and a supporter of Megan Lloyd George, who was the Member of Parliament for Anglesey, and had been since 1929. I knew that it would cause some difficulties, but I went home and told my parents. I'd

ON THE HIGHER LEVEL

qualified as a solicitor at the beginning of the war and my father said, 'You haven't even proved you can earn yourself a living, what right do you think you've got to become a Member of Parliament?' I said, 'Well, let me think about it.'

In the end, I accepted the invitation and when I was able to come home on leave again in a few months, I met the party, in the home of one of them, over a cup of tea. They asked me to say a few words; why I'd become a candidate, what did I think of the Labour Party, what did I think of this, that and the other. I gave a little talk. And that was that; I got adopted and, in due course, the election came in '45, and I applied for leave of absence from the Air Force and I came home and fought it.

Flying Officer CLEDWYN HUGHES (Labour, Anglesey)

✖ Three months before the election I had no intention of standing for Parliament. I was commanding a Mosquito squadron in France about fifty or sixty miles north-west of Paris and I had worked for Beaverbrook and the *Express* newspapers between university and the start of the war. About four or five weeks before the Armistice on Luneberg Heath I had a letter from John Gordon, the editor of the *Sunday Express*. He simply said, 'An election is going to follow the end of the war in Europe very smartly and Lord Beaverbrook thinks that one or two of the younger people in the organisation who have been through the war and survived ought to consider standing for Parliament. Your name's been mentioned. How do you feel about it? He said, 'Politics is a dirty business but, if you're interested, which party would you support? Tell me what your intentions are and we could start the ball rolling from here.' So I acknowledged the letter, but I didn't reply for a fortnight or three weeks. To tell you the truth I hadn't even thought about standing for Parliament.

There was no one to talk to in the wing. No one knew the first thing about politics and cared less about it, and I couldn't make up my mind whether to do it or not. Anyway, the Armistice came and I still hadn't made up my mind and, quite by chance, the Commander-in-Chief of the Second Tactical Air Force sent for me and said, 'I want to have a good record written of the operations of the tactical Air Forces, of which I am the commander, from the Battle of Alamein to Berlin. Now Lucas you're just the fellow for it.' Gill and I had just met and I thought I bet that's an eighteen months' job at least. I thought to myself, well there's only one thing to do and that is to play for time. I said to him, 'Well, sir, I've been out here since September and I haven't had any leave, not even a forty-eight-hour pass. Would you mind if I took a week's leave in London and gave you an answer at the end of it?' 'Oh,' he said, 'certainly. Take ten days if you like, there's no hurry.'

So I got into a Mosquito, and on the way back I did my calculations. I thought to myself, well that's eighteen months and I'll probably be all over the bloody place. If I stand for Parliament that's a three-week campaign. So I made up my mind that I would go and see John Gordon at the *Express*. He said, 'Well, it took you a long time to make up your mind but you'd better go along and see them.' I went in to see the Chairman of the Party in Smith Square. He said, 'All the seats have gone. The only thing I can offer you is Limehouse against Attlee.' And he sort of paused for a moment and I didn't make any reply, so he said, 'Well, you say you're thirty, well yes, that's about right. Put up a good show if you go there, and in four years fight a better seat, then you'll be thirty-four. That's about the age to get into the House of Commons.'

I said OK. He said, 'You'll have to get down there tonight. I'll send the name down.' So I went down there and I went into the office. There was no organisation, no agent, nothing. Absolutely hopeless.

I then got home and the telephone bell went. Gordon from the *Express* on the line and he said, 'They tell me that they've offered you Limehouse against Attlee. This is absolutely ridiculous. We'll have to do better for you than that. Just give it a day. Don't do anything. Take it slowly.' So, anyway, the following evening he rang up again and he said, 'We hear that the candidate in West Fulham is not going to go on and Lord Beaverbrook's sister, Jean Stickney, lives in Fulham. I think we've got a bit of pull there.' So, the long and the short of it was that I got on the short-list in Fulham and on the short-list was Lucas, Freddie Erroll, who's in the House of Lords now, and a fellow who was a brewer.

All the halls in Fulham were bombed, so we had the selection meeting of the full executive in a church. I remember the room was absolutely full of women – practically no men at all – and they'd all got hats on. They all seemed to have ornaments on the tops of their hats. So whenever you made them laugh, everything sort of shook. Anyway I got them shaking. That was the great thing. And I got the nomination. Well, I go and get beat by seven thousand or something votes by Edith Summerskill; Freddie Erroll went up to Altrincham and he was there until they sent him to the House of Lords. I was beaten by seven thousand votes.

Wing Commander LADDIE LUCAS (Conservative, West Fulham)

WHAT THE ELECTION WILL BE ABOUT

BRITAIN'S coming Election will be the greatest test in our history of the judgment and common sense of our people.

The nation wants food, work and homes. It wants more than that – it wants good food in plenty, useful work for all, and comfortable, labour-saving homes that take full advantage of the resources of modern science and productive industry. It wants a high and rising standard of living, security for all against a rainy day, an educational system that will give every boy and girl a chance to develop the best that is in them.

These are the aims. In themselves they are no more than words. All parties may declare that in principle they agree with them. But the test of a political programme is whether it is sufficiently in earnest about the objectives to adopt the means needed to realise them. It is very easy to set out a list of aims. What matters is whether it is backed up by a genuine workmanlike plan conceived without regard to sectional vested interests and carried through in a spirit of resolute concentration.

Point by point these national aims need analysis. Point by point it will be found that if they are to be turned into realities the nation and its post-war Governments will be called upon to put the nation above any sectional interest, above any cheap slogan about so-called free enterprise. The problems and pressures of the post-war world threaten our security and progress as surely as – though less dramatically than – the Germans threatened them in 1940. We need the spirit of Dunkirk and of the Blitz sustained over a period of years.

The Labour Party's programme is a practical expression of that spirit applied to the tasks of peace. It calls for hard work, energy and sound sense.

We must prevent another war, and that means we must have such an international organisation as will give all nations real security against future aggression. But Britain can only play her full part in such an international plan if our spirit as shown in our handling of home affairs is firm, wise and determined. This statement of policy, therefore, begins at home.

And in stating it we give clear notice that we will not tolerate obstruction of the people's will by the House of Lords.

The Labour Party stands for freedom—for freedom of worship, freedom of speech, freedom of the Press. The Labour Party will see to it that we keep and enlarge these freedoms, and that we enjoy again the personal civil liberties we have, of our own free will, sacrificed to win the war. The freedom of the Trade Unions, denied by the Trade Disputes and Trade Unions Act, 1927, must also be restored. But there are certain so-called freedoms that Labour will not tolerate: freedom to exploit other people; freedom to pay poor wages and to push up prices for selfish profit; freedom to deprive the people of the means of living full, happy, healthy lives.

The nation needs a tremendous overhaul, a great programme of modernisation and re-equipment of its homes, its factories and machinery, its schools, its social services.

All parties say so – the Labour Party means it. For the Labour Party is prepared to achieve it by drastic policies of replanning and by keeping a firm constructive hand on our whole productive machinery; the Labour Party will put the community first and the sectional interests of private business after. Labour will plan from the ground up—giving an appropriate place to constructive enterprise and private endeavour in the national plan, but dealing decisively with those interests which would use high-sounding talk about economic freedom to cloak their determination to put themselves and their wishes above those of the whole nation.

from 'Let Us Face the Future', published by the Labour Party – April 1945

CHAPTER THREE

Fighting the Good Fight

The 1945 election was the end of the old politics: twelve university seats, nine two-member constituencies, three-party politics, no television, and newspapers thinner and distracted by war. Radio broadcasts were few – ten for each major party, four for the Liberals and one each for Common Wealth and the Communists. Churchill did a four-day tour, but national tours by major figures were much less important, and the routine of spin doctors, press conferences and image enhancement was totally unknown. So everything focused on the constituencies. Six hundred and forty campaigns fought by 1,683 candidates – 622 Tory and allies, 603 Labour, the greatest number ever, and 307 liberals. Each fought in their own way.

This was a candidates' campaign. Party organisation was reviving, memberships small, activists fewer than usual though each had a pent-up energy and more began to emerge.

✘ When it came to the election the Labour Party came out of nowhere. We knew who they were but had not identified them as Labour, yet they became the hub of the Labour Party in 1945 and for a long time after.

FRANK CLAYTON

Central help and guidance were minimal, pamphlets limited by paper-rationing, so candidates were free to improvise and most were learning on the job. The candidates' contest became a political outward-bound course with so much to be crammed into so little time if they were to reach out and re-enthuse the electorate and kick-start the motor of politics.

✗ There is an extraordinary difference between campaigns then and now. I was not conscious of any interference from Transport House. We fought our own election. We were isolated. There weren't all these quantities of leaflets or instructions or things you ought to concentrate on.

I came back from the Navy from a fleet where there was some resentment – certainly disgruntlement because people had forgotten in Europe that we were fighting the Japanese. I didn't know what the domestic issues were and I thought up my own slogan for the election which I plastered all around the place, 'We built the Spitfires. Now we can build the houses', which I thought was a good rallying cry. It was extraordinary because my election agent Bill Headon, who had been born and bred in the constituency and knew everybody, had never been known to smile in his life, and yet I found that a smile was occasionally creasing his face. That was a clear indication we were going to win by a large majority.

For transport we had one car, which was loaned to me by a local printer, and a box tricycle. That was appropriated by the chairman of the party who was the driver on the Great Western Railway express from Cardiff to Paddington. He used to ride around in this with the box on the tricycle full of leaflets and we used to distribute them. It was the most amateurish campaign you could possibly think of. We had no records; there was a rudimentary party in some of the wards but there was such tremendous enthusiasm.

We held meetings outside the shipyards, and every night, of course, three meetings a night, and they were all crowded and they were all tremendously enthusiastic.

Lieutenant JAMES CALLAGHAN (Labour, Cardiff South)

✗ I was fighting this odd constituency in Yorkshire which started at Pudsey which was an old Liberal mill-owner's seat, and then went from the Aire Valley past Harry Ramsden's, the fish and chip shop, into Wharfedale. In the Wharfedale area we had a very big membership in Otley. We had a very active support in Ilkley which was really like Cheltenham in a way, a middle-class spa town.

The thing I most remember about it was it was a wonderful summer so of course going up into the little villages of Wharfedale was a very pleasant experience. But it was still the age of the squirearchy and I will never forget going to one village, I think in the Washburn Valley, just above Otley, where nobody would come out to a meeting. So we put our van in the middle of the village

An election? I don't beleve it!

green and spoke. Everybody listened to us, but in their cottages round the green behind the curtains. They were so frightened of upsetting the squire.

It was a wonderful experience, colossal enthusiasm and as I say lovely weather which always helps. I had to borrow a car from two old maiden ladies at Bramham and I remember it breaking down so I had an awful job getting home to Keighley that evening. But the enthusiasm and idealism was extraordinary. I had eleven meetings starting at 6 p.m. and finishing at 11.30 p.m. Can you imagine speaking for about five to ten minutes at each? It was all public meetings and nothing else and a lot of answering questions. The halls were packed and very enthusiastic, but then as now the overwhelming majority of people who went to meetings were committed to the party of the chap who was speaking. There were always a few obligatory hecklers sent by the opposition. So you didn't really get a lot of chance to get at the so-called floating voter, I don't think.

Major DENIS HEALEY (Labour, Pudsey and Otley)

✘ We hadn't much of an organisation. A bit but not much, but what it lacked in numbers it made up with enthusiasm. I was fortunate enough to be helped by people who believed in something.

I campaigned in uniform, in view of the fact that I was standing in a naval constituency and it was solidly naval. I put that point to my own executive and, indeed, to the public meeting at my adoption. I said, 'Look, how do you want me to be.' They said, 'We'd prefer you in uniform,' and an officer at that, which, in a prospective Labour constituency was probably regarded as a little unique. So there I turned up, rank and all, brown job, major, Sam Browne, the lot.

You didn't have to bother about *Coronation Street* being on, so you could have meetings in the evening plus, of course, walking the streets. And that's what I did in the main. I was preceded by a loudspeaker and I would stop at various points. I must have spoken in most streets in the whole of the north constituency of Portsmouth. But there were the big meetings as well, and they were very well attended in those days. I remember speaking at a meeting in the Central Hall in Portsmouth. There must have been a couple of thousand. Mainly good-humoured heckling but some of it well timed and some of it planted. It was a classic political campaign as I knew it in the old days. Very exhilarating.

Major DONALD BRUCE (Labour, Portsmouth North)

✘ I was absolutely exhausted because of course we had had the war and just at the end we had had the V1s and then the landmines and your sleep was interrupted. I went down with a severe attack of shingles and looking at the photographs of that campaign I can see how drawn and white I was with the stress of war.

None the less the atmosphere buoyed one up because there was such excitement and such enthusiasm. Our eve-of-the-poll meeting in St George's Hall, Blackburn, which was a very large public hall, was crowded. There were three thousand people there. Every seat occupied, they were lining the walls, they were hanging over the balconies, and there was a sort of unbelievable buoyancy in the atmosphere, as though people who had had all the textile depression years, the men and women who had suffered in the forces and the women who had been working double shifts, making munitions and the rest of it, suddenly thought, 'My heavens, we can win the peace for people like us.'

That faith carried one along through all one's physical fatigue and I have never experienced before or since anything like the atmosphere of that meeting.

BARBARA CASTLE (Labour, Blackburn)

✘ During the war, I had evacuated my wife and children to Bournemouth and our house in London had been completely destroyed, so we had no London residence to work from. The local

Conservative organisation had no money. They didn't even have £5 in the kitty and I had to raise some finance which wasn't very easy. For the first time in my life I had to get a mortgage, on my destroyed house to finance my own campaign. I must say though that when I ultimately gave up the constituency because the practice had become busy at the Bar, the local organisation re-funded me a good deal of money.

Commander F. ASHE LINCOLN (Conservative, Harrow East)

✘ I was in the Air Force and I was selected as prospective candidate for the Chislehurst constituency. On the face of it, it was a pretty hopeless job. When the election came I got released from the forces, but although my wife had kept the constituency going during the war, we only had about £10 in the bank; nevertheless we spent money right, left and centre, hoping to get it in. We did, because we used the National Dried Milk tins used for my baby son at that time, and we put Labour Party bills round them and we collected money that way. In addition, I had hundreds of pounds shoved through my door.

We'd got hardly any party members and during the campaign in the rural area we hadn't got any representation at all so I adopted a new idea, very unconstitutional. At the end of our meetings I called for volunteers to form a good Labour Party committee. Anybody at all was welcome, and slowly but surely we built up a whole party organisation, campaigning with people from the audience.

Dartford Rural District was a tremendous area and I had an amateur agent. He had to work during the day, so during the day I was agent and candidate. We had a little old van which was run by a chap that hired his loudspeaker to us, and I was sitting in the back on a chair tied to the bed of the van by a rope as we careered all round the constituency. When we finished the campaigning we came back to my home because the Labour Hall had been burnt down in the March – a deliberate act on somebody's part – and we had to use our house. My agent came and lived in our house. We'd go to bed about 11.00 p.m. and get up at 6.00 a.m. to deal with the postage, fill all the addressed envelopes and so on, to get them out to the constituents. Then he'd go off to work and I'd set off campaigning during the day. It was a hit-and-miss affair but the fantastic meetings I had were incredible. The chap with the loudspeaker was a bit of an asset because he could climb trees and whilst we were canvassing he was climbing the trees in the rural

Abingdon: D. H. Parkinson, Labour candidate

area nailing up posters on the trees so we had quite a good campaign there.

I did six eve-of-poll meetings in the evening in a huge area stretching from Sidcup right down to Gravesend. When I came to my last meeting the school hall was in darkness but the place was packed. All I said was, 'Ladies and gentleman, we're going to win,' and then my voice completely went and I was unable to speak for about a day until it came back again. Then, of course, we had to wait for the vote to come in from the forces. I went back to my old firm who very kindly gave me a job for the time being because money was a bit short.

Sergeant GEORGE WALLACE (Labour, Chislehurst)

✘ I was the youngest candidate in the country. The sitting Labour member for Chester-le-Street was Jack Lawson, an ex-miner, simple, courageous, a great gentleman who in theory hated Conservatives but in fact liked nearly everybody. I had met him several times and knew he was unbeatable.

My constituency lay south of Newcastle, north of Durham and was a coal-mining area. I was told I would have a bad reception. My relations remembered with pleasure my grandfather fighting a Durham seat in the 1880s. He was cut in the face by a snowball filled with glass. I was too excited to be discouraged and began my election campaign. Masses of literature arrived through the post. Central Office advised candidates to take the line that Churchill, having won the war, should be given a chance to 'finish the job'. I soon realised this idea would not go down well in Chester-le-Street. At every meeting at the beginning of the campaign I was reminded the Prime Minister had once declared he would like to 'shoot the miners', He had also been Chancellor of the Exchequer during the strike of 1926 and was responsible for the means test, etc., etc. In other words our suggested card was a liability.

The market town of Chester-le-Street, a couple of miles away from where I lived, had a number of Conservative voters and a Masonic Lodge, donated by my family. I was informed I could rely on a hundred Masonic votes! It was, therefore, decided that my wife and I should use it as the starting place for our canvassing campaign. I hated the idea, but even in the poorest houses, to my surprise, I was politely received. No doors were shut, although husbands asked what I knew about life, when I had never been down a pit; they laughed when I said I had. I was never abused and several housewives treated me kindly and said, sadly, 'It is a shame to make a poor laddie like you start working so early.' The words 'poor laddie' were repeated so often that I soon realised the Labour plan was to treat me as a joke, not as an adult. I was annoyed. I had begun to think of myself as a young statesman, taking the first steps of his distinguished career.

It was no use pointing out that I had wanted to stand. The aristocracy, they believed, was a villainous union whose loyal members had to be trained in the art of ruling the country to their own advantage. I found with a couple of drinks I could make speeches and it was not difficult to meander on, despite my cold reception when I said Mr Churchill had won the war and that the country had been brought to ruination by the Labour government of 1929–31. Then I would point out to scanty audiences how the Foreign Secretary, Mr Eden, was a 'Durham man', and how every child should be educated up to the age of sixteen; also that we planned to build new houses, maintain the Empire and so on. The truth is, anyone except an idiot can make a political speech at a General Election.

Viscount LAMBTON (Conservative, Chester-le-Street)

Come on, Archie!

Cmdr. Sir Archibald Southby, in his adoption speech as Conservative candidate at Epsom last night, said:

"If when I die I am remembered for nothing else, I hope I shall be remembered for having saved the land opposite the grandstand from being ploughed up during the war so that you can have racing here once more."

Newspaper cutting, 16 June 1945

✘ I've just been looking at my diary for that year and I find that I did eighty public meetings in the three weeks of the campaign. Which is not bad considering that I also did a lot of daytime functions that I didn't class as meetings but just part of the routine. There were problems with transport. Petrol was on a coupon system and candidates and their election agents were allowed extra coupons, but the ordinary helper hadn't got an excuse. We tried to help out as much as we could so the speaker who was at the furthermost point took out all the other speakers for the series of meetings and dropped them off one at a time. When the last speaker had finished he collected the others to bring them back. It was a risky business because the candidate didn't always arrive back on time, and there were some problems, but we only left out the coroner for York; he'd come to give me a hand so we had to take him out and, unfortunately, we left him. We had a roll call every night to make quite sure that we hadn't left anybody out.

We would have won this constituency if we'd had more cars. First, there weren't many cars available, secondly, there was such an awful lot of people in need of transport and, thirdly, we just couldn't get enough petrol for what cars we had. So we had people in remote villages waiting to be picked up by what cars we did have. We just couldn't get them in. And we only lost that election by a hundred and sixteen.

BERT HAZELL (Labour, Barkstone Ash)

✘ The first difficulty was to find an agent. The first agent that the Conservative Party got for me knew nothing about electoral laws at all and he arranged a whole series of meetings in public houses. So we had to scrap all that and get rid of him as quickly as possible. Then we did get another young man to act as agent but when I went up to start the campaign the total paid-up membership of the Conservative Party in that constituency, where there were 80,000 voters, was only a hundred.

Commander F. ASHE LINCOLN (Conservative, Harrow East)

✘ It was only a relatively short campaign but I had been a candidate for nine years. I had a long relationship as a prospective candidate and I had a very strong Liberal press. The *Salisbury Times* gave me an enormous amount of coverage. I did a thousand words a week for about six years so I was quite a well-known person in the constituency when I was fighting it.

Very friendly meetings. Tremendous turnout and terrific enthusiasm. John Morrison was the Conservative candidate. He fought me very cleverly. He said what a very nice fellow I was and that I was so nice I really ought to be a Conservative. He tried to kill me with kindness. I refused to go and have dinner with him in the election. The Labour Party had a brigadier and he wasn't a particularly strong candidate.

We had quite a strong organisation, including the editor of the *Salisbury Times* who was a very powerful supporter. We weren't short of organisation and we went all round. Salisbury and South Wilts was a very big constituency. We had ninety villages and we had a very large area to cover. I delivered a hundred and forty speeches in the campaign, and I estimate that as I spoke for twenty minutes probably every time, I was on my feet for forty-eight hours, so it was a very arduous campaign.

Wing Commander ALAN CAMPBELL-JOHNSON
(Liberal, Salisbury and South Wiltshire)

No time to change horses!

We've got a figure-head – we've got an Admiral – and if nobody notices we haven't a ship we shall be OK!

✖ In Bournemouth we were pretty isolated from the rest of the country so we were starting out completely from scratch. We hadn't fought the seat since 1929. We started out with one active person – the constituency organisation was as dead as a doornail – but he was a very remarkable chap. He was my chairman and he became the honorary agent. A fellow who wrote thrillers. His name was John Creasey. He had a very vivid imagination and a very good sense of PR in the days when I don't think anybody had ever heard the words 'public relations'. He decided at once that the only possible way we could fight was to make it a publicity campaign, there was no hope of having any organisation. What we had to do was make a noise. And we made one hell of a noise.

He knew the local paper, the *Bournemouth Echo*, very well. They adhered to their policy of being independent but said they would give publicity according to which candidate happened to make the most news. We made news. He was very, very good at creating opportunities for newsmaking. We spent the days loudspeakering around the place, making a hell of a noise. Bournemouth Square gets thousands of people in it on a summer's Saturday. He would station his loudspeaker van at one end and I would station mine at the other end of the square, and he would toss questions across to me over the heads of the people, and I would answer them. Then he would invite people to come up and talk to him. He would then put their questions to me, and I would answer them. It went down very well.

We had a devil of a lot of meetings. We agreed to hold two meetings in each ward. I can't remember how many wards there were, but it meant about five or six meetings a night. We advertised them in the local press and by bellowing out on the loudspeaker that we were coming round that evening.

We managed after about twenty-five phone calls and telegrams to get Archie Sinclair, who was our leader, to look in on his way to somewhere else. He had an absolutely jampacked meeting somewhere in the town, thousands of people. The national swing really passed us by altogether. There was no swing to Labour in our seat. I was a young subaltern who had come out of the army. My election address had a picture of a very handsome young man in uniform, needless to say. The Labour chap, a very nice fellow called Robert Pollard, was a Quaker who had been a conscientious objector during the war. We wouldn't, of course, make any play of that, obviously not. They would tell people they mustn't be put off

Abingdon: Big Cars vote Tory

by the fact that the Labour candidate had been a conscientious objector, whereas the Liberal candidate had been fighting gallantly for his country.

Lieutenant BASIL WIGODER (Liberal, Bournemouth)

✘ My opponent was a fellow named Plug and he had a poster up, 'Plug for Churchill', so I put a poster up, 'Pull out the Plug, and let the Tories down the drain'. Herbert Morrison came to speak for me, and there was a circus at the Chatham Empire where Morrison was going to speak. So my agent arranged with the circus that when Morrison was speaking they'd get one of the lions to roar. The lion roared and Herbert Morrison said, 'Go and stop it, Arthur.' So I went, stopped the lion roaring and when I came back Morrison said, 'What a King of the Lions you are.'

It was a very exciting campaign. My star attraction was Sybil

Thorndyke. Her husband got her to join the Labour Party and she came to speak for me. It was a very emotional speech. She begged the dock labourers, who had some food left, to give it to her to give to the hungry children. She borrowed some old sheets and tore them up and made them into bandages for sufferers. She was really a remarkable person. The Corn Exchange where she spoke was where she had first acted as a schoolgirl so it was a great occasion. Nearly all the audience were schoolgirl fans. So it was a great success.

There were meetings everywhere and, being a dockyard town, the sailors turned up in strength, and they used to shout out to my wife, 'come on, you talk for him'. But they were very good, more exciting meetings than we have today. Violence wouldn't have been known in those days. We were carried away with the enthusiasm.

ARTHUR BOTTOMLEY (Labour, Rochester and Chatham)

✘ I was completely new to the art of campaigning. I suppose one learns about it by the art of doing. I was thrown in at the very deep end. Harold Lever, who was then Lieutenant Lever, was the candidate in the adjoining constituency of Cheetham, and we started off with an open-air meeting in a park just inside his constituency but serving both constituencies, where I had for the first time to speak in the open air. It seemed to go down and one picks up from then on. However, the enthusiasm at that time towards Labour candidates was such that you didn't have to say anything really. You just had to be there. One word and everybody clapped and said, 'Hear, hear!' It was just like that in 1945. There were a large number of meetings and they were very well attended. You had gatherings outside the favourite pubs where people would congregate, especially on the eve of polling, just to cheer.

JACK DIAMOND (Labour, Manchester, Blackley)

✘ I really loved the campaign. It was quite rough, a lot of heckling. They turned over my car one night. That was in the market square, quite late. We'd been to four or five meetings a night in those days, and perhaps they'd had one or two drinks. Anyway it didn't come to any harm and it was the greatest possible fun. My wife simply loved it. It was all canvassing, and four or five meetings a night. One of the worst slums in Chesterfield was called Cavendish Square and has now been

Herbert Morrison shows the way to the lions' cage

pulled down. That wasn't so good. They were very good at the factories and I went down a coalmine and had myself photographed down there. We went to all the big factories and the works owners arranged for me to have a hearing. I got a fairly good grilling, but it was all pretty good natured. I think they thought I was pretty odd. They were very friendly. They are marvellous people in Chesterfield. Real good people, and I used to tease George Benson, my opponent, and say he was a carpetbagger from Manchester. You should vote for a Derbyshire man – all that kind of thing. It was pretty childish but I enjoyed it anyway.

I remember one heckler who said, 'You lot all travel first class, and we all travel third class,' and I said, 'You vote for me and we'll all be travelling first class.' Coal nationalisation was very much an issue and, though my family have done well from coal royalties, luckily we didn't own any coalmines. So there was no family issue on that. I had a group of hecklers who'd come round with us meeting to meeting. I got very friendly with them, and it was nearly always the same questions so, after a bit, you got to know the answers. It's very much easier to answer a question than to ask one.

Lord ANDREW CAVENDISH (Conservative, West Derbyshire)

A Brief Note for Fabian Speakers and Canvassers in the Election

The Electorate: It should be realized that we have to make an appeal this time to two different sections of electorate.

(1) The service elector, who, in the main, is quite divorced from the actual political conflict in his constituency and will have no direct communication, except the candidate's election addresses. (Urge all relatives and friends to send literature or local papers to service voters.)

(2) The ordinary domestic voter, who has hardly recovered from the relief of VE Day and who, in many cases, would have liked more time to sort ideas out before deciding issues of the election.

In both these groups there are, in my view, two similar characteristics:

(a) Both types of voters are, in the main prepared for some kind of political change. They are tired of voting for the rich or society candidate. This attitude, shown in the West Derbyshire election when the electorate rejected the Marquis of Hartington, has been a recurring feature of every by-election since. The important point is to establish confidence in the Labour movement's ability to bring about change without causing chaos.

(b) There is a considerable amount of political cynicism. The men and women in the forces quite properly posed the question – 'What Government has ever kept its election pledges?' A quite similar saying from the doorstep is – 'Well, its all the same whoever gets in!' – and – 'They are all out for themselves anyway.' In my view, the only successful counter to this psychological feeling is to emphasise not only the personal importance of the individual's vote but also to show him that there does exist a positive plan in the movement for the solution of our economic and social problems; in this connection, I think that vituperation centring round the record of one's opponents is about the worst method of winning the support of the non-political voter. Obviously some proportion of propaganda must be devoted to the unsatisfactory record of the Conservatives in the eighteen out of the twenty last years between the two wars during which they had power, but I make it a rule, myself, never to devote more than 10% of energy to more 'record breaking'.

Arthur Skeffington

JOHN WILMOT'S
DEPTFORD
ELECTION SPECIAL
General Election, July 5, 1945

Candidate's Address

THURSDAY—
THIS WAY
VOTING, JULY 5
7 a.m. till 9 p.m.

| WILMOT | X |

Under the counter. Is it to be the same story as at the end of the last war? Do you remember? A trick election, then a Tory Government. Controls off! Prices and rents rocketing! "Homes for Heroes" promised but never built! Chaos and unemployment! Is it to be the same again?

Here are pictures of what actually happened then. Plenty for the rich! Queues for the poor! It is beginning again. Are they holding up supplies in the hope that if the Tories win, price control will come off? Think it over!

Necessities first. A better way than the Tory way of leaving it to private profit, with "black market" and "under the counter" methods is the "LABOUR WAY" of making sure that the people get the food, houses and furniture they need at the prices they can afford to pay. This means organizing the production of necessities first, and it means also the control of prices and materials, and the key services such as transport and power for the use of the public.

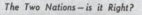

The Two Nations — is it Right?

Don't let them divide us into two nations— Rich — and — Poor

Cock Robin, Daily Express, 24 May 1945

✗ My folks lived at 40 Millbank along here just where the Millbank Tower now is. I was twenty and too young to vote, so I drove a loudspeaker van. The Labour candidate was somebody called Jeremy Hutchinson, who is now a peer, and his wife was Peggy Ashcroft. I drove Peggy Ashcroft around throughout the election and she would get out of the loudspeaker van and address the people in the Peabody estates about the need for a National Theatre.

We had our headquarters in Victoria Street, at the Civil Service Housing Association. We did marvellous things, I drove to Covent Garden and I drove into a taxi. Now normally if a Labour vehicle drives into a taxi you would think it would cause trouble but I got out and said on the loudspeaker, 'You have just been struck by the Labour candidate,' and everybody cheered – they were so excited. And then Knocker O'Connell, who was one of the bummeries from Covent Garden, gave us a political alphabet. It went on interminably but I do remember one of the verses: 'F stands for freedom,' said Knocker, 'what Britain brags about. If you can't afford your dinner you're free to go without.'

We canvassed No. 10 Downing Street, because Jeremy Hutchinson was a lawyer. It was before the Thatcher gates and all that, but there were guys in tin hats and sandbags and bayonets and Jeremy turned up and said, 'I am a Labour candidate and I have got the

Register and there is somebody living at No. 10,' and they let us through. So we knocked on the door of No. 10 and the whole domestic staff came out. It was just like *Upstairs, Downstairs*. There was a butler in the front and he said, 'We are all Conservative in this house,' and a little maid in the back in a bonnet said, 'We'd lose our jobs if we weren't.'

TONY BENN

✗ It was a very short, very vigorous campaign, with very crowded school meetings. In those days we had loudspeakers which we would mount on the top of a car. I was let loose from the pits, where I was a Bevin boy, for a fortnight for this campaign – no more. It was very exciting. I remember twelve senior pit lads came to London to help. We housed them all in the borough and all they did was go to every pub in the place and drink every lunchtime and every evening. These twelve chaps just talked to everyone: talked about the pits and Jack the lad – they called me 'Jack the lad'.

I had a campaign organiser, an agent appointed by the London Labour Party. Will Webster. He was a real huckster of a campaign organiser. It was all noise and cheering. Every schoolhouse had a full meeting for that area, and there would be someone to shout, 'Here he comes. The candidate. Here he comes.' People would be a bit surprised but, eventually 'Hurrah, hurrah', and they would be persuaded to join in the excitement of the candidate appearing. It was utter nonsense and, of course, can't exist now with the 'box' and everyone being guided by that.

JOHN PLATTS-MILLS (Labour, Finsbury)

✗ My election agent was a young coalminer who'd had an injury in the pits. He was a violent anti-Communist and there were a lot of them about at that time. He set me forth on his programme of election. Talk about slavery, it was political slavery that he put me through. Three weeks of it. Morning, afternoon and night on loudspeaker, public meetings, pit meetings. It was the most exciting election I've ever been in. I've contested everyone from '45 to 1987 and I've never had one like that.

I fought Gallagher in 1945 and in 1950 and never a word passed between us, and never a handshake. The Communists regarded West Fife as their hereditary right, and they threw everything at me. It was, I think, the only election at that time where physical violence was the order of the day. The knuckle-duster, the fists, and we had some of the best fighters in our women's section. I remember a village in the middle of the coalfield where the Communists had their headquarters, and they defied me to go in there and have a public meeting. So Willie Marshall and others said, 'We're bloody well going.' We couldn't get the halls because the Communists had complete control. So we said we'll have our platform on the top of an air-raid shelter, and the Bevin boys in a neighbouring village, big lads, said, 'We'll be your bodyguard, Willie.' So they sat with their legs dangling over the side of this concrete air-raid shelter. I was stood on the thing and gave my speech, and when the Communists were trying to climb on they were pushing them back with their feet and crushing their bloody fingers.

It went on like that for the three weeks with physical violence in meetings and outside. The Communists were painting the streets and painting everything that stood still with their slogans.

Lieutenant WILLIE HAMILTON (Labour, West Fife)

✘ It was an extraordinary campaign. To be quite honest for the first fortnight we thought we were going to win. Beaverbrook came to speak for me twice and I could always get these first-class names because it's so close to Westminster. The second time when he came down, four or five days before the eve of poll, he said, 'News is very bad in the country. News is very bad. Going down badly. Old Winston,' he said, 'is depressed and he's making these silly speeches. What are your canvassing returns like?' To be honest I didn't know what the bloody canvassing returns did look like. I can always remember at the end of the meeting old Bill Berkley, who was the parliamentary reporter on the *Express*, said, 'As for the Conservative candidate it's quite clear that he's still far more at home in the cockpit of a Spitfire than he is on a political platform.'

Beaverbrook spoke in a sort of biblical English, 'And then it came to pass that Baldwin came to power.' The noise in West Fulham in that election was terrific. Packed meetings and all shouting away. I didn't mind that, I thought it was quite fun actually and Beaverbrook always spoke first. He stirred it up and ruined it for me. A fellow was heckling away saying, 'Who let the beaver out of the brook?' It stirred the old boy up, and he eventually said, 'My friend, my friend, you want the platform. Come over here.' I mean can you ever imagine anyone asking a heckler to come up on to the

Lord Beaverbrook   *Mr Herbert Morrison*

platform? 'If you send him back to Westminster I'll eat my hat.' And Beaverbrook picked his cap up and he said, 'He's going to eat this, ladies and gentleman,' and there was a bloody great shout.

Jill's brother-in-law, Douglas Bader, was back in the Air Force, and I asked him to come up and speak. He came up one evening with about twenty or thirty of these guys, all in uniform, though Douglas wasn't. The hall was packed, probably between two hundred and fifty to three hundred people in the hall, and outside a couple of thousand. The chairman was no good and lost control of the meeting. Douglas started in on some curious tack. He didn't know anything about politics any more than I did, but he said, 'I speak for the candidate. I don't mind which party he's a member of but I speak for the candidate,' and he said, 'I know this guy . . . ' and some chap from the back of the hall got hold of a copy of King's Regulations and started to quote these blooming passages, about serving officers speaking on political platforms. Douglas managed to get through it because of the goodwill which was there, but these fellows who had come up with him from Tangmere were all shouting at this chap, 'Keep quiet.'

Wing Commander LADDIE LUCAS (Conservative, West Fulham)

✖ In Birmingham I was advised that the less they saw of you the more likely they were to vote for you. I noted that when people were ill during a General Election campaign they got a much higher vote than the surrounding area for their particular party. It is not a view generally accepted by constituency parties, who believe the more you're seen the better it is. Particularly untrue.

I remember one broken-down house, the door was hanging off, almost collapsing, and I approached this house with great confidence and banged on the door – 'I suppose you'll be voting Labour?' 'Go on, Get away! You don't even believe in the Union Jack!' and the chap threw me out!

Major WOODROW WYATT (Labour, Birmingham, Aston)

✘ I said to my agent, 'You know Monday is Selby Market day? Book me a stall, because if you start speaking without having rented a stall you might get shooed off.' So we rented an ordinary stall on Monday afternoon before the date of the election, and I'd just got started when up came Colonel Whatnot with a whole entourage of cars and people. I'd noticed that the stall next to me wasn't occupied but assumed that the owner had gone home. I had the usual little tannoy which wasn't much good, but it helped – they weren't very efficient in those days. He'd got a high-powered speaker. He jumped on to his stand, and I was on mine, and there we were blaring it out, one tannoy against another. I don't think the people understood a word of what we said, either of us, but they enjoyed it. It was a most hilarious meeting. He had wrecked mine, but I had wrecked his.

BERT HAZELL (Labour, Barkston Ash)

✘ There hadn't been a General Election for ten years and I found that the country people down there were not politically active. There was virtually no organisation, none of the parties in the rural places had an organisation. In the towns the Labour Party had kept the organisation going in the war but the Conservative Party hadn't really got much organisation anyway.

The people were amazingly ignorant of party political affairs then, but the evening meetings that I held were terribly well attended. Quite large halls absolutely packed with people out of sheer curiosity. The interesting thing was that the issues that were discussed didn't concern socialism much. 'How quickly can we get the boys home?' was the main issue and many people thought that Winston Churchill would be Prime Minister whatever party won. It was not a hostile campaign.

Major DAVID RENTON (National Liberal, Huntingdonshire)

GENERAL ELECTION, 1945.

BARKSTON ASH PARLIAMENTARY DIVISION

THE LABOUR CANDIDATE,

Mr. BERT HAZELL

STANDS FOR :—

The complete defeat of Japan.

A World Organization to keep the Peace.

The Public Ownership of the Bank of England and key industries.

Strict Public Supervision of Monopolies and Cartels.

A Prosperous Agricultural Industry—giving a fair return to farmers and farm workers.

A Housing Drive—until every family has a well-built home.

The Best Education to give all Children a fair start in life.

A National Health Service.

Early Legislation extending Social Security to All.

Adequate Old Age Pensions without the Means Test.

Give Labour Power—Vote for Hazell

Printed by Delittle, Fenwick & Co., Ltd., Railway Street, York.
Published by Frank Smithson, J.P., 94, The Green, Acomb, York.

Lord Buckhurst, Conservative at Bethnel Green

✘ There were two constituencies next door to each other and Percy Harris had been the member for Bethnal Green for donkey's years and they absolutely loved him down there. He was a great character and a splendid man in many ways. I was adopted for the next door one which I think was a Labour seat but I suppose they thought if we ran it in tandem it wasn't a hopeless seat by any manner of means. It was hopeless for the Tory, obviously, and he lost his deposit. The sitting member was a trade unionist who's name I simply can't remember now; not at all a very exciting person. He got back quite comfortably but I think I gave him a run for his money. The campaign went on for about three weeks as far as I can remember and my agent, who was a very professional agent, sensibly kept me as far away from the platform as he dared because I was easily bowled over by a good question.

I spent my time canvassing. I simply went from door to door all round the place and that was a marvellous experience because they're absolutely terrific people down there. I campaigned in uniform. There's a picture of me looking about fifteen, I suppose, taken in a pub down there.

There was an active Liberal organisation there. The chairman was a road sweeper, the secretary or one of the other people was a very prosperous fishmonger, and I spent some time touring round in the back of his fish van with a loudspeaker. I had a set speech and trotted that out, but it was the questions that rather floored me. I don't think I'd have made a good Member of Parliament actually. I've always though it was providential that I wasn't elected.

Major PAUL WRIGHT (Liberal, North East Bethnal Green)

✘ My husband and I went one evening for a walk, because I was pregnant and needed a walk. I remember seeing a huge election poster for Churchill, and some East Enders tearing it down. My husband said to me, 'Now that is what you should not do in a democracy. In a democracy you fight elections and you respect one another, and you do not tear the posters down.' So we got a bit nearer and one turned out to be a Czech and the other a Pole, and they were both socialists and they were not having Churchill. We tried to explain it to them.

IRENE WAGNER (London Fabian)

✘ A week before polling day I was invited to attend a meeting of Catholic priests in the area and found myself in a closed room being hotly pressed to undertake the work which they wanted done on Catholic schools. I didn't react very well, I'm afraid. (a) I was new to the job and, therefore, hadn't learned the art of saying anything other than what was on my mind, and (b) I resented being put in a closed room without any others there. So I suppose I was a little bit brusque in my dealings with them. I said I would consider it, or words to that effect. Two or three days later, from every Catholic pulpit on Sunday morning, those attending were told not to vote for me, specifically by name, because I wasn't satisfactory with regard to the all-important question of Roman Catholic schools. I had to put out a pamphlet the following day. However, the good people of Blackley listened to what their priests had to say, and voted Labour.

JACK DIAMOND (Labour, Manchester, Blackley)

✘ Maurice and his wife Katie came to stay at weekends to get away from their gloomy lodgings in Seaham. He inadvertently did me a bad turn by saying a mutual great uncle of ours, once a distinguished politician, had in the early years of the century a devastating method of dealing with hecklers. He would ask them up on the platform to make a speech. Horrified and flustered they would collapse and look silly. I liked the idea and decided to try it out at my next meeting. The chance came when a little mousey man kept interrupting me. I asked him to step up. He smiled, accepted and gave for five minutes a lucid explanation of Labour's policy. I, blushing, sat looking idiotic. He was applauded. I found myself clapping his speech.

Another near calamity occurred on the first Saturday. Tired out, I drank two glasses of whisky before going to the meeting. At the chairman's house I was given what he called a 'stiff whisky'. By the time I reached the platform I was drunk, and could only sit smiling, unable to stand up. It was said I was ill. I continued to smile. Curiously enough, Jack Lawson told me years later my drunkenness had got round the constituency and done me 'no end of good'. But at the time I felt miserable and never again had more than one drink before a meeting. During the first week I was so busy trying to get my speech right I did not think much about national politics. During the second I began to see that the audiences were unimpressed and questions became more national than personal.

Viscount LAMBTON (Conservative, Chester-le-Street)

✗ Very few people had transport and I remember I found that addressing the bus queues in Huntingdon, St Ives and St Neots I had captive audiences. So I spent a good deal of my time addressing bus queues. In the mornings I would visit factories and markets. It was a huge farming area with three market mornings a week. Then I would visit factories, mainly up at the northern end.

In the afternoons I would do three villages and the people were out at work on the farms so one couldn't see many people, but in the evenings I would have three meetings in village halls and places and a final meeting always in one of the urban areas. It was a very, very strenuous campaign.

On the morning of the poll, 5 July 1945, I stayed in the George Hotel, Huntingdon. To get to the town hall I had to go past the church, which sticks out into the old North Road which ran through Huntingdon High Street; I was running and I didn't realise, because I wasn't as familiar with the place then as I became, that there was a buttress of the church leaving only a foot to go past. As I ran past I hit that buttress and fell down in the road and a lorry had to swerve to avoid killing me. There was jolly nearly a by-election before the election started.

Major DAVID RENTON (National Liberal, Huntingdonshire)

✘ I didn't know much about Solihull issues. I'd never been there until four or five weeks before polling day. On an entirely nepotistic basis I got Attlee to come and speak for me. No basis on which he ought to have come with a rational allocation of the party leader, because there was no way in which I was going to win. My father was his PPS and a great friend of his. So he came. It was a good Attlee speech, by which I mean it was a fairly flat speech but delivered crisply, and one was very glad to have him along. But we had quite a lot of speakers.

Kingsley Martin I remember coming and speaking for me. Austin Albu, later chairman of the Fabian Society. He came and spent the whole last week of the campaign with me.

It was an active campaign all right. We had long light evenings, but it was a campaign mostly of very well-attended meetings. Typical meetings would be in the main hall of the school, therefore there would be seats for about a hundred and fifty to two hundred people, and normally there would be another hundred people standing round the edges. I hardly recollect a single badly attended meeting, and we had a certain amount of open-air stuff, but not a vast amount. Occasionally, after a meeting, we'd go out and have a thing outside a pub and people would gather round. I remember seas of faces looking up in the twilight, a mixture of exhaustion, hope, some kind of doubt. A sea of tired faces looking up in hope, that's the best phrase I can make of it.

Captain ROY JENKINS (Labour, Solihull)

✘ I was doing a personal canvas as far as I could of the constituency and one of the constituents was Clement Attlee. So I boldly called on his house. He answered the door, and I said, 'Well, Mr Attlee, I'm the Conservative candidate and I know it's no good asking you for your vote.' He laughed, so I said, 'May I see your wife?' So he said, 'Certainly, come in,' and he made me very welcome and I sat and talked to her. I said, 'I can understand that you would want to support your husband, but let me assure you that, first of all, the poll is absolutely secret and, secondly, the question you have to answer is, "What is my duty to my country?" So I would suggest, if you don't mind, that your duty to your country is to vote for Churchill.' They were all very amused, but I got out safely anyway and remained on quite friendly terms with Attlee ever afterwards.

Commander F. ASHE LINCOLN (Conservative, Harrow East)

✗ I didn't think in terms of winning or losing when the election got going. I just became confident we would win, in my seat as well as in the country. It was a strange election because the Tories relied on Churchill and Churchill, I could see, was not a favourite of the working man in Manchester. They thought that he had enjoyed the war more than they had, and that war was an exciting thing for him. He got a very doubtful reception when he came on a tour to Manchester and there were as many boos as cheers.

I'd never had any doubt I was going to win. My photograph was shown in all the houses, and there was a distinctly Jewish area in my constituency in 1945, and there the voting was about ninety-eight per cent in my favour. Not because it was me, because I'm a Jew, but because the Jews were always Labour Party voters. So I soon saw that I was going to win the election and my agent didn't believe me. Terrific campaign. I must have made about a hundred speeches in the schoolrooms, in the streets. It was packed at every meeting in the schoolrooms, and every meeting in the streets was crowded. I've never made so many speeches in an election as in the '45 election.

Flying Officer HAROLD LEVER (Labour, Manchester Exchange)

✗ I was suddenly told that none other than the Prime Minister, Sir Winston Churchill, was prepared to stop off and speak for a short time whilst on his way to St Andrews and Dundee. I immediately arranged to hold an outdoor meeting on the courtyard of the town hall at Linlithgow. We were mercifully blessed with a lovely sunny day, and a worthwhile crowd soon collected when they heard the Prime Minister's voice over the loudspeaker. I recall he began his speech slowly, in a low-key manner, but he soon warmed up and, as he did so, he started waving his arms about, whispering to me 'take it, 'take it'. At first I did not appreciate what 'it' was. Then mercifully the penny dropped and I realised he was referring to his famous hat. Not quite a top-hat, nor a bowler-hat – I don't think I have ever seen a similar hat – but Winston was fond of it and he wore it a lot; so I grasped it and enabled him, unencumbered, freely to wave his arms about and deliver his address.

For the only indoors meeting which I held during the campaign I managed to persuade that great character and Lord Provost of Edinburgh, Sir Will Y. Darling, to come over to Linlithgow to speak for me. We had an indoor meeting in a very full hall and he didn't half stir things up. The war having only just ended and being near several naval bases on the Firth of Forth, there was a strong contingent at the meeting from the Rosyth Dockyard and elsewhere; also many soldiers, awaiting demobilisation. I remember the meeting gave Sir Will Y. and myself fair and reasonable attention, but then the service personnel got going – mainly, to my surprise, to attack each other. I recall one sailor in uniform shouting out, 'I belong to a Tory service and you lot don't know what you are talking about!' All that Will Y. and I had to do was sit back and enjoy ourselves.

Colonel RUPERT SPEIR (Conservative, Linlithgow)

✗ Churchill was splendid except for one notorious speech in which he said that, 'If we have a Socialist government it will be like having a Gestapo.' That didn't go down well. I made a joke of it in Huntingdonshire and found that other people made a joke of it too. Rather giving the impression that he'd intended it as a bit of a joke. Whether he did or not I don't know.

Major DAVID RENTON (National Liberal, Huntingdonshire)

✗ The Astors had a London house in Upper Grosvenor Street and it was open house at lunchtime. I used always to go there at lunchtime and there was always Anthony Eden or someone else there. I could always hear someone saying, 'Well Anthony's going to say this in Huddersfield tonight and someone else is going to say that.' I thought, well, I'll get that down and tell them in West Fulham.

Bill Astor had got old Winston to come down and speak for us in East Fulham. Bill, being East Fulham, got into the back of his car first and it stopped outside our committee rooms in Fulham Road and he beckoned to me. I got up on to the back behind the old boy and Winston, with his great tall bowler, was standing up in the front there, acknowledging the crowd. Bill said, 'This is Wing Commander Lucas, sir,' and he grunted.

So we moved on. Probably two or three thousand people there and he lifted the thing absolutely; and the thing that impressed me so much about him was that he used short words and commonplace words and somehow they had a different meaning. Then he got to the end and he was saying, 'And so, ladies and gentlemen, I commend to you two fine fighting candidates – Mr Bill Astor who has already served you in the House of Commons and, here in West Fulham, another fine fighting candidate – what did you say

WINSTON CHURCHILL'S FIRST PARTY POLITICAL BROADCAST, BBC, 4 JUNE 1945

Socialism is, in its essence, an attack not only upon British enterprise, but upon the right of the ordinary man or woman to breathe freely without having a harsh, clumsy, tyrannical hand clapped across their mouths and nostrils. A Free Parliament – look at that – a Free Parliament is odious to the Socialist doctrine . . .

No Socialist Government conducting the entire life and industry of the country could afford to allow free, sharp or violently worded expressions of public discontent. They would have to fall back on some form of Gestapo, no doubt very humanely directed in the first instance. And this would nip opinion in the bud; it would stop criticism as it reared its head, and it would gather all the power to the supreme party and the party leaders, rising like stately pinnacles above their vast bureaucracies of civil servants, no longer servants and no longer civil. And where would the ordinary simple folk – the common people, as they call them in America – where would they be, once this mighty organism had got them in its grip? . . .

your name was again?' And Bill said, 'Lucas, sir, Wing Commander Lucas.' And he said, 'Much obliged,' then he said, 'And so, as I say, we have these two fighting candidates here, Bill Astor whom I've mentioned, and – what was that name again? – another fine fighting candidate in West Fulham.' Anyway, Bill got off then and I went through the blooming constituency up to Putney Bridge and got off, and got on to a 14 bus. Tuppeny ride, and I was back at the headquarters again. Politics is a very humbling business.

Wing Commander LADDIE LUCAS (Conservative, West Fulham)

✘ I think we were somewhat critical of Churchill during the campaign. We thought he went over the top. He was Beaverbrook's mouthpiece rather than Churchill's mouthpiece. But of course, in Lancashire, people who voted Labour thought they were voting for Churchill. Lots of them, particularly old ladies. When I went to his big meeting in Preston, in the castle there, there were masses of people who came to see him and he arrived weeping tears because

CLEMENT ATTLEE'S REPLY, BBC, 5TH JUNE 1945

When I listened to the Prime Minister's speech last night, in which he gave such a travesty of the policy of the Labour Party, I realised at once what was his object.

He wanted the electors to understand how great was the difference between Winston Churchill the great leader in war of a united nation and Mr Churchill the party leader of the Conservatives. He feared lest those who had accepted his leadership in war might be tempted out of gratitude to follow him further. I thank him for having disillusioned them so thoroughly. The voice we heard last night was that of Mr Churchill but the mind was that of Lord Beaverbrook.

I am also addressing you tonight on the wireless for the first time in five years as a party leader, but before turning to the issues that divide parties, I would like to pay my tribute to my colleagues in the late government, of all parties or of none, with whom I have had the privilege of serving, under a great leader in war, the Prime Minister.

It is on domestic policy that we get the main clash between parties. The Prime Minister spent a lot of time painting to you a lurid picture of what would happen under a Labour government in pursuit of what he called 'a continental conception'.

He has forgotten that Socialist theory was developed by Robert Owen in Britain long before Karl Marx. He has forgotten that Australia and New Zealand, whose peoples have played so great a part in the war, and the Scandinavian countries have had socialist governments for years, to the great benefit of their people with none of these dreadful consequences. There are no countries in the world more free and democratic ...

there was a cold wind blowing. He made a fighting speech and got a tremendous hand. You would have thought Preston's all right, but it wasn't. But I think one knew that feelings towards the war leader were different from feelings towards the Conservative Party leader.

Brigadier A. R. W. LOW (Conservative, Blackpool North)

✗ You can't see Edmonton now as it was. It was long streets of working-class houses and a lot of them had been put up by the borough. It was Labour, and they knew how to run their local community, they were very efficient. The campaign was very exciting too because this very efficient organisation had booked all the main meeting halls. The town hall was always booked by the Labour Party. They gave the Conservatives one night there, and the Liberals another night. The rest of the week was all Labour.

It was unbelievable, people were pouring into the Labour meetings. People relied on the *Daily Herald* and what they read in there. They put their cross on the papers on the day but they didn't know why, except that they were trade unionists or their grandfathers had told them they must.

It was tremendous. Wherever we went it was, 'Vote Labour'. Ted Cole, the agent, arranged that my husband should be shown to the electorate and that he should get to as many of the thoroughfares and side streets as he could, but not go to every door because that's very tiring. They hired or acquired a Morris Oxford 14, a big family gentleman's car and very nicely upholstered inside, but it had seen better days. We filled this with all the ladies who wanted to help the Labour Party; five, six or seven of them would pile into this car. I had a loudspeaker calling, 'Your candidate, Evan Durbin, is now in your neighbourhood. If you would like to come and talk to him he is available at the end of the street. If you cannot come we will take him to your door. Vote Labour.' Evan went down to whoever wanted to be spoken to, but they all came out of their doors when they heard us.

We had it all mapped out exactly which area we would go to. We had some of Evan's students down from London to help. With the Labour ladies and the LSE students it was quite a mixture. They would make me go round and do the Labour women and the churches. I do remember the Methodist church ladies because they asked me quite intelligent questions. Most of them, I would say, were Liberal voters and even in a gathering like that the Labour people didn't want to speak up.

MARJORIE DURBIN (Widow of Evan Durbin MP)

✗ The issues we fought on were primarily Beveridge, who was a Liberal of course, fighting the election himself, though he lost his seat somewhere or other up in the North. Jobs for all, houses for all, health for all; one could promise anything in those days, quite

We will vote for our Eirene

We will vote for Our Eirene,
    Yes! indeed,
We will vote for Our Eirene,
    Yes! indeed:
We will send her to Westminster,
Our clever "Young Welsh Spinster,"
We will vote for "OUR EIRENE,"
    Yes! indeed.

The Tories will be crying
    Ow! Ow! Ow!
The Tories will be crying
    Ow! Ow! Ow!
Yes the Tories will be crying
We hear that Nigel's sighing
Because his Party's dying,
    Ow! Ow! Ow!

William Hughes your Party's
    Dead! dead! dead!
William Hughes your Party's
    Dead! dead! dead!
William Hughes your Party's dead,
So come over to the Reds,
William Hughes your Party's
    Dead! dead! dead!

Published by A. G. Moyle (Agent), 115, High Street, Connah's Quay
and Printed by Edwin Jones and Son, 9, Argyle Street, Wrexham.

cheerfully and without regard to anybody asking you to cost your programme. Foreign policy didn't seem to play any part in the election that I can remember. I remember Leonard Lyle, who was the Tory candidate, was very pro imperial preference, and I used to have a go at him on that, on free-trade grounds. Otherwise I don't think there was any mention, that I can think of, of international order after the war. We talked about strengthening the League of Nations, International Police Force and so forth, that was about as far as it went.

I had a look at my scrapbook this morning and was appalled to see a copy of my election address which would reduce you to hysterics if you saw it. It showed on the front this young man in uniform; it was written by John Creasey not by me, and it was really written as a thriller. I remember the opening lines were – I'm ashamed to repeat them – 'As I lay in the trenches outside Casino I thought of the causes of war and the men dying around me . . .' something like that . . . but once you'd started it you couldn't actually put it down until you got to the end. He was a very gifted writer.

Lieutenant BASIL WIGODER (Liberal, Bournemouth)

✘ It was a hell of a good programme and I loved it. You could talk about the national insurance scheme that was going to come in, and the old folks were going to get a good increase in their pension, and the free health service. I'd got a pair of glasses. I promised folks that they would be getting free glasses and free false teeth and that, and they were rubbing their hands. As for the miners. There were fifty pits in that constituency and I said to them, 'You'll own those pits in a couple of years. You'll own all those pits.'

Lieutenant WILLIE HAMILTON (Labour, West Fife)

✘ The men out there in the Far East wanted to be demobilised as quickly as possible and they had written home to tell their mothers and their sweethearts and their wives, 'The best ways you can get us demobilised is not to vote for that warmongering Churchill but to vote Labour, they will get us out of the army.' So I found a tremendous cry for that, both from the fathers and mothers and from the men themselves. So I was riding a popular wave with no idea of the difficulties we were going to face. I had been away out of the country and was quite out of touch with all the worries that were besetting ministers up here. I'm sure I would promise the earth. I had no reason not to do so. So I wouldn't care for all my speeches made in that election to be known about now.

Lieutenant JAMES CALLAGHAN (Labour, Cardiff South)

✘ The Churchill factor was a very complicated one because I think a lot of people were very confused because there had not been an election for ten years. They didn't think of him as a Conservative, I don't think. I went canvassing in one of the very badly hit parts of the East End and in a very left-wing bit, a place called Russia Lane, well named I might say. The door was opened by an old lady with a man's cap on, with a pin through it, and she looked at me very hostile. She said, 'Who are you?' so I said, 'I'm the Liberal candidate in the election.' 'Oh', she said, 'you'd better come inside, young man.' So I went in. She shut the door and we stood in the hall and she said to me, 'Now, young man, you look like a nice young man to me so I'm going to advise you to bugger off from here. We've always been Labour in this house and we're voting for Old Churchill.'

Major PAUL WRIGHT (Liberal, North East Bethnal Green)

Packed meetings: Coventry

✘ My campaign was 'Back Churchill'. A Derbyshire man, 'Back Churchill'. I didn't expect to win but I didn't think I would get beaten by as many as I did, and I think that is because on a campaign you naturally only see your own supporters. They are loyal to the absolute hilt and you only hear the good news, and I thought I was going quite well. I'd got a dentist friend in the car and I had a drink with him one night and he said, 'Don't be under any illusion. You're going to be very heavily beaten.' I was a bit surprised, but I really knew on polling day. It was fine, and very hard work getting voters in and going to the polling booth, and then, when the factories shut, suddenly you could see these thousands and thousands of workers and they weren't going to vote for me. That was quite clear. By five o'clock in the evening, I realised then.

Lord ANDREW CAVENDISH (Conservative, Chesterfield)

✘ At the end of polling day we certainly thought we were running the Tories very close, and we thought Labour had lost their deposit. We'd absolutely no organisation on polling day. We'd got, I think, paper tellers at the committee rooms – what they were telling us, I've no idea. They just took lists of numbers and went home and had tea. There was no suggestion of any knocking-up operation or any canvassing or anything of that nature. Then we got to that extraordinary period of the three weeks before the forces' vote was cast. I must say, during those three weeks I never had the slightest inkling there would be anything other than a Tory win nationwide. It never occurred to me that Labour were going to get in. What was going to happen to the Liberals I didn't know either. I thought we'd do rather better than we did, but the idea that Churchill would be rejected as a result of the election never crossed our minds at all.

Lieutenant BASIL WIGODER (Liberal, Bournemouth)

✖ On election day itself they got a truck and they painted it all red. Evan and I went round his constituency all day long, standing on this truck. I had a beautiful new suit which I'd bought in Liberty's sale, and damn me, the paint wasn't dry. I ruined it leaning against the rail and they were horrified at lunchtime when they saw this. We were going round in this truck all day. My husband didn't like any of this activity. He called it just cheering and wasting time. He preferred it on the campaign, when he could speak to people. He was very serious in his politics but he hated all this tomfoolery.

Before the poll closed at nine o'clock we were in one of these long streets just going round with a whole lot of cars, and there were people hooting and tooting. We'd say, 'Have you voted, have you voted?' We were pushing them to vote, and the poor things, they didn't want to chase up to the town hall to vote. They thought it was enough to shout 'Good old Labour'. It was great fun but Evan kept saying, 'Oh my God, they haven't voted yet.' And it was unnecessary because he had this vast majority.

MARJORIE DURBIN, Widow of Evan Durbin MP

✖ During the last week my father and stepmother came down to hear me speak in the market place in Chester-le-Street. They were taken up to the second floor of a shop and given seats in front of a plate-glass window. Unfortunately only its top quarter opened. This suited my father but my polite stepmother, wishing to hear me put her head through the narrow gap and could not get it out. It was difficult to make a speech and at the same time watch two men pulling a fat stepmother's head back into the shop. Everybody was sorry about the incident. It was not thought to be funny.

Viscount LAMBTON (Conservative, Chester-le-Street)

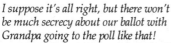

I suppose it's all right, but there won't be much secrecy about our ballot with Grandpa going to the poll like that!

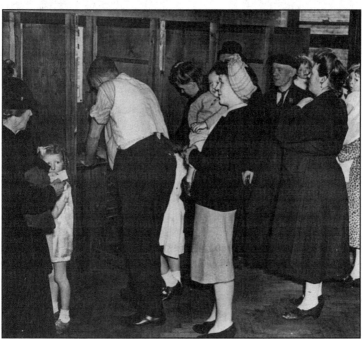

Polling Day, 5 July 1945 – nine years, eight months since the last General Election

Lord Marchwood   *Raymond Jones*

CHAPTER FOUR

Waiting and Wondering

Polling on 5 July ushered in a three-week lull. Campaigns packed up. Candidates went back to what they'd been doing before. Activists rested. The reconstituted Coalition carried on, transferring the war effort to the East, preparing for the Potsdam Conference to start on 17 July, with Britain represented by Churchill, Attlee and Eden. Only in nineteen constituencies did the fight go on. There the election had been postponed because of Wakes Week.

✖ In Nelson & Colne we didn't have our election until three weeks later because of the Wakes Week. In those days the Wakes Week was more important than little things like elections. It meant that everybody had finished their elections so they all converged on Nelson & Colne because we were the only one still to go. Among the people that came to help me was Randolph Churchill, who had been a bit of a friend although he was a bit of a washout really because he always made truculent speeches. He brought a pamphlet which showed that Sidney Silverman had signed a peace pamphlet within twelve months of the war starting. So I challenged him to a great debate in the ballroom. The young Lieutenant, active Young Conservative, against this very able parliamentarian who was absolutely left and on top of that a pacifist.

Winston Churchill came along too. He didn't quite know where he was, you know, with these tours, and Nelson & Colne was the border between Lancashire and Yorkshire. So when I got to sit with him in his coupé while we were going to the Burnley football ground, where he was going to have his mass meeting, he said, 'Where am I? What town is it now?' I said, 'You're in Lancashire now. We've just come into Lancashire.' When he was making his great speech on the football ground he referred to, 'You good people of Yorkshire . . .' I said, 'Lancashire!' whereupon he made a

DAY AFTER

quick recovery – 'of Yorkshire's neighbour, the great Lancashire, blah blah blah . . . ' He got out of that beautifully.

The other thing that was rather interesting on that bit of the tour was seeing the great man getting out to have a pee behind the hedge. And at the side of the road, which was crowded, one old chap as he went past was saying 'Boo'. You'd normally ignore it but Winston, he'd got his normal cigar hanging there, he turned round and said 'Boo' back. It was all very human and very good.

Lieutenant HARMAR-NICHOLLS
(Conservative, Nelson and Colne. Defeated by 8,126)

Meanwhile the forces' vote came in – 986,784 by proxy, 1,032,688 by postal ballot. Parties and candidates waited for counts and declarations on 26 July. Most assumed this would confirm Winston Churchill in power.

✘ We worked hard on 5 July, but did not celebrate beyond saying, 'Thank God that's over.' In the early evening of 25 July the ward agent called and invited me to a victory celebration at a nearby union HQ and club. I wondered how we could celebrate the night before the count. It seems that on 25 July in Stratford, and I assume elsewhere, the ballot boxes were taken to the town hall and the ballot papers counted to reconcile the number with the number issued. Thus anyone present could see which way things were going. I have always wondered why the result next day apparently took Churchill and the press by surprise. Surely impressions as to how various constituencies had voted were fed back to party HQs?

ARTHUR EDWARDS

✘ We didn't really expect we could win; John Edwards and I, who were fighting seats with a five thousand Tory majority, thought we would scrape in probably, with a bit of luck. But nobody in the Labour Party expected the landslide that happened, except Aneurin Bevan, who had some sort of political antennae which told him there was a ground swell of discontent. All right, Churchill may have won the war, but they'd never forgotten what he did in the peace. What a bruiser he was, a right-wing politician whom we wouldn't trust to win the peace.

We had this awful waiting period after the closing of the polls with the domestic vote, waiting for the votes from the forces to come in. And then we found we had got a majority of eight thousand each, a dramatic swing which seemed impossible because Churchill confidently believed he'd walk it to power as an act of national gratitude.

BARBARA CASTLE (Labour, Blackburn.
Second place with 35,145 votes in a two-member borough)

✘ The count took place in a hotel on the seafront at Southsea, because the Guildhall itself had been bombed pretty severely during the war, and we had the count under the benign eye of the town clerk, who's name was Blanchard. It never occurred to me that I wasn't going to win, but I knew it was going to be narrow. I think Julian Snow's count finished first. Captain Julian Snow who afterwards became an official in the government, some kind of Gold Stick. He got back with a reasonable majority. So I thought well, yes, we stand a chance, and we did, of course, even though it was quite narrow (it was a little over a thousand). It obviously surprised the Tories.

What I did note was when we went to the Mayor's Parlour afterwards I was completely isolated from the old people in the council, because it was mainly a Tory council, largely building

contractors, second-hand car dealers and petrol station owners –
those were the bulk of the councillors. So they succeeded in
freezing me out at the celebrations afterwards. Except for Greville
Howard who, ostentatiously, came across and we had a chat
together. When they saw Greville Howard had broken the ice, they
all came up.

Then I addressed the admiring populace on the steps of the hotel
on Southsea front. I shocked my own supporters, I think, by
suggesting we should be a little wary in victory, because every
victory contains within itself the seeds of its own defeat as, of
course, ultimately it did. It was an hilarious occasion, everyone
enjoyed themselves. I did not get drunk that night but I had an
adequate amount of alcohol suitable to the occasion. I felt pretty
good. I wasn't surprised by the national result. There were two
people who I think were not surprised. One was Aneurin Bevan
and the other was myself.

Major DONALD BRUCE
(Labour, Portsmouth North, Majority 1,042)

✘ Well I had never seen such a turnout in all my life. I should say
about ninety per cent of the forces' vote was for me, and one chap
put two rounds of ammunition in with his vote, one each for my
two opponents. The returning officer very kindly allowed the vote
but pinched the ammunition. I don't know what he did with it. I
had as my opponent Major Nigel Fisher, who was a real gentleman, no argument about it, and General Hawkins was the Liberal.
We got on well and on polling day General Hawkins came along
with plenty of chocolate and kept my wife and me fed with
chocolate during the count. But believe it or not we turned the vote
round and I got in by over six thousand.

Sergeant GEORGE WALLACE (Labour, Chislehurst. Majority 6,279)

✘ The most extraordinary time was the count, which we held in
a schoolroom just outside Guiseley. My pile of votes was rising
with the Tory pile until it really looked as if I might win, but in the
end we didn't quite do it. We reduced the majority of 12,000 to
1,600, but I never expected to win it. But the wonderful thing was
that last hour, when finally my Tory opponent's votes started
rising faster than mine, we got one Tory bigwig after another being
tumbled. I remember Macmillan's defeat being announced on the
little portable radio I had and that made up for any personal

Ernest Bevin re-elected in Wandsworth

disappointment. It was an extraordinary experience and oddly enough I would have won if I had had a good Liberal opponent. If the Liberal had got as many votes as he had in '35, I would have been home and dry, but unfortunately the Liberals chose a chap who had been the army heavyweight boxing champion called Brigadier Terence Clark who later became a Tory, and the nearest thing to Neanderthal man in the House of Commons, as the MP for Portsmouth.

If he'd been any good I would have won. It was a very odd election because we were all three ex-service and I was the lowest rank: I was only a major. Then there was this chap who had been the army heavyweight boxing champion, Terry Clark, and then Malcolm Stoddart-Scott who won the Pudsey and Otley seat. He'd never served abroad because he was a pox-doctor and he had plenty of work to do at home.

Major DENIS HEALEY
(Labour, Pudsey and Otley. Defeated by 1,651)

✖ The mood of the country was very friendly to people who had been fighting so I don't think I was out of touch with the feeling of the country. Having read the papers and having listened to what people said, I didn't think Labour would win by a majority of two hundred but I thought it would win. I was surprised actually how well we did in Blackpool but I think that was like Lancastrians – they are much more open, so you could tackle their grievances more easily. I think, looking back to 1939, I didn't actually feel that Neville Chamberlain was going to win an election in 1939. You have to remember that I thought I was going to win personally. I was nervous for the first week, but after we did a lot of canvassing there were a few sour faces, but not a lot. It felt good.

Brigadier A. R. W. LOW
(Conservative, Blackpool North. Majority 12,394)

✗ I had a majority of five thousand in an electorate of only 39,000 people over twenty-one so I was very pleased. When I heard my result, I thought, 'By Jove, we are going to have a tremendous win nationally.' Then I came down from the balcony of the town hall at Huntingdon, where I had been required to make a speech thanking everyone for voting and thanking the returning officer and all that, and blow me somebody came up and said, 'It looks as though the Labour Party have got a tremendous win.' Then we went and had lunch in the local hotel, the chairman and the Conservative chairman and the agent and my parents and we turned on the radio and we found that it was so. A tremendous socialist win.

It felt very strange but we thought and hoped and believed that under Attlee it would be a moderate socialist government. It wasn't, it nationalised everything.

Major DAVID RENTON
(National Liberal, Huntingdonshire. Majority 5,931)

✗ I was carried literally shoulder high from the city hall almost before the speeches had been concluded, my supporters were so enthusiastic. There were men and women there with tears in their eyes. It was so unexpected, I don't think we had really imagined a victory of that sort. It was the consummation of so many hopes and aspirations over such a long period and here we seemed to be on the point of achieving it all. I recall going into the local hotel at lunchtime, 12.55 p.m., and the 1 o'clock news came on, and sitting in the corner unknown and isolated because he didn't belong to Cardiff and nobody knew him was the Secretary of State for War, Sir James Grigg, who had been elected in a by-election for Cardiff

East against Fenner Brockway in about 1942 or so. As the news came through on the 1 o'clock bulletin it seemed inconceivable to hear these impregnable names of Tory ministers toppling one after another, cut down like trees in the forest as they crashed to the ground. When the name of Sir James Grigg came over the air, as they read out this list of names, there was a group of young army officers sitting in the other corner. They didn't know Grigg. They didn't know he was there, and instinctively they shouted with a loud 'Hoorah!' and there was the poor man, literally without anybody with him because all his campaign people had gone.

Lieutenant JAMES CALLAGHAN
(Labour, Cardiff South, Majority 5,944)

✘ During elections, candidates are inclined to persuade themselves they are doing well and will cause a surprise result, and I remember at the beginning persuading myself there could be another 1931. But reality soon returned. The results of the election at Chester-le-Street were not announced on polling day. By the next morning it was known that Attlee was in, Churchill out. At the count, Jack Lawson had a faraway look in his eyes. After my congratulatory speech, I said, 'I hope he will get the high office we all know he deserves.' Afterwards he took me aside, thanked me and said, 'You're not a bad lad, you know.' I was by now totally fed-up with all this ladding, but was pleased by his friendliness. Having won ten thousand votes, neither been stoned nor molested nor made a total fool of myself as some of my relations had prophesied and doubtless half hoped I would, I had done something. It had been amusing. I had enjoyed myself.

Viscount LAMBTON
(Conservative, Chester-le-Street. Defeated by 23,560)

✘ We got to Newcastle about 11 o'clock this morning and our result was declared at 12.30. The figures were self, 17,381; Shackleton 10,228; McKeag 5,812; Ridsdale 904. It was a great relief – and a famous victory in this truly catastrophic election – never was such a crushing disaster – the three other Newcastle seats have gone and, except for a victory at Berwick where Beveridge was turned out, we have only one other seat in the whole northern area – Penrith & Cockermouth. It is the same story all over the country. Labour has a clear majority of a hundred and fifty or thereabouts over 'the rest' – Winston has resigned and little Mr Attlee reigns instead – it is a sorry business and one feels ashamed of one's countrymen. But there it is, this is democracy – the people wanted a change and, no longer being afraid, voted Labour. The left-wing propaganda has had its effect and it would seem that the vast majority of the new generation has gone Socialist for the time being. What a House of Commons it is going to be – filled with young, half-baked, young men, mainly from the RAF so far as I can make out.

Parliament and Politics in the Age of Churchill and Attlee: The
Headlam Diaries 1935–51, Stuart Ball (ed.), to be published in 1996

✖ When the election came I had lost by six hundred and forty-two votes and had it been different my life would have been utterly changed. Had I won I would have been a Liberal MP, probably the youngest Liberal MP, and I suspect I could have ended up, as such was the possibility for Liberal MPs, as leader of the Liberal Party. Washed out, finished, without a penny in the world, instead. Beaverbrook, when I fought my second election, said to me, 'Well what is it going to be here? politics or journalism? If it is politics you will reach the highest echelons. If it is journalism I will put the golden crown on your head.' I had a kid at the time, and another on the way, and my total capital was about £100 and I was living in a tied cottage. So I said, 'journalism'.

Lieutenant JOHN JUNOR (Liberal, Kincardine and
West Aberdeen. Defeated by 642)

✖ It was a morning count three weeks later, to let the service vote come in. That did produce less tension that a late-night count. A long time to keep up tension. I don't think I went into that count thinking I was going to win and therefore I don't remember a great shock of ebbing hope and the result wasn't overwhelming, it was probably one of the smallest Tory majorities there's ever been in Solihull. But then of course the national result came out gradually over that afternoon and that was sensational. That was superb. Tremendous sense of exhilaration, I suppose on my part tinged with just the smallest hue of disappointment. Four hundred Labour MPs had been elected. I hadn't managed to be one of them. None the less at twenty-four you couldn't expect too much. But it left me very determined to get into the House of Commons as soon as I could. It took me a while after that, another two years and ten months. But that wasn't too bad.

Captain ROY JENKINS (Labour, Solihull. Defeated by 5,049)

✘ The history of Barkston Ash wasn't one that would make you highly optimistic that you were suddenly going to change the world. But we went to the count with a fair amount of confidence. We'd had a good run, we'd put up the vote – we knew that because of the degree of enthusiasm. After all there aren't many candidates who could say that they were going from Garforth to Knottingly and were stopped on the road by a town band and told, 'Now look, you get on the roof of the car, we're going to lead you into Knottingly for a meeting.' They were so enthusiastic that the drummer broke the head off his drumstick and he had to finish the march thumping with his fists.

We got to the count at Selby, and when the first run-through had taken place and they were sorting them out, I said to my agent, 'This is going to be close Frank.'

When we got the final figures and there were only a hundred and sixteen, my agent said to me, 'What are you going to do about it – ask for a recount?' I said, 'There's only got to be one bundle switched from one side to the other and we're home.' But it didn't turn out like that. We were thoroughly pleased with the result yet we were saddened in one way because we knew that we'd had people on polling day who lived just too far away to walk. There were no cars to take them. They'd stood and waited for hours, hopeful that someone would pick them up. This happened all throughout the constituency.

BERT HAZELL (Labour, Barkston Ash. Defeated by 116)

✘ In the jargon of the day we lost a battle but we won the war, and that was the most important thing. My immediate problem after we'd lost was that I didn't have the bloody fare to get back to my wife when we'd just had a baby, two days before the result was announced. That was my consolation prize, my daughter, two days before the result. We'd already arranged a victory social. I told them that I had no ruddy money to get back to see my wife and daughter. They had a whip round at this social and collected me about three quid which was my fare, single fare down from Fife, from Edinburgh to Whitehaven.

Lieutenant WILLIE HAMILTON (Labour, West Fife. Defeated by 2,056)

✘ We were all brothers and shook each other's hands and generally departed in a state of goodwill. My mother, who was a realist and didn't think I ought to go on in politics, said that my party was too much in love with losing. She said that there was too

"MAKE WAY!"

much of the moral purity; that sense of rectitude which comes from being in a permanent minority. My mother didn't care for that. She said, 'You're there to win and you can't go on doing this, you've got to earn a living and look after your family.'

I had other things to think about. I was in South East Asia Command. Three days after the result of the election I was at Broadlands where Mountbatten had just come back from the Potsdam Conference with the staggering news that there was going to be an atom bomb dropped and we were not going to invade Malaya. The war was going to be over, and he was going to take charge of the whole of South East Asia and we were going to be put in charge of Indonesia. All these considerations were very much in my mind. So I didn't have very long to mourn the result.

It was an incredible period. You think about it. The election, then the Potsdam Conference, and then the atom bomb dropped on the 6 August. Within a week. Staggering events. Mountbatten said, 'Nobody will believe what I'm telling you. We're not going to have to fight this war. It's going to be over.' We were planning operations for another two years. So my mind was on other matters, if you understand me.

Wing Commander ALAN CAMPBELL-JOHNSON
(Liberal, Salisbury and South Wiltshire. Third place with 8,946 votes)

CHAPTER FIVE

Shock Waves

All morning on 26 July, BBC bulletins carried the news of the fall of ministers and Labour's toll of seats mounted. By the lunchtime news it was clear a great victory was in the offing and the final figures showed that Labour had made 209 net gains to win 393 seats on 11,992,000 votes. The Conservatives were reduced to 189 seats and 8,666,000 votes. The Liberals were a rump of twelve MPs, fewer than ever before and fewer than the independents. Labour had a majority of 146 over all other parties, more than enough to build the New Britain. All over the world supporters rejoiced.

✘ I spent 26 July on a flight across the Atlantic. The pilot passed round a message – 'First results show Churchill relected.' Was this a garble for 'rejected' or 're-elected'? The huge headlines in New York removed that doubt. Then came anxious questions from Americans about the meaning of the result, and for me a belief – alas naïve – that never again would there be a Tory government in Britain.

DAVID JONES (London Fabian)

✘ In July 1945 I was in Sarajevo as chief of the Bosnian office of the UNRA mission to Yugoslavia. We had a staff that consisted mainly of British medical personnel and of Yugoslav secretaries, interpreters and liaison staff. On the day when the General Election results in the UK were being counted we had with us also a film unit from the UK, headed up by Arthur Calder Marshall. Most of us had been in Italy, and before that, in Egypt, and some of us had been involved with the Forces' Parliament in Cairo. It was our view that if – and we regarded this as a big if – the forces' vote from overseas got through to be counted, then Labour would be re-turned. All of us, including the Americans and Yugoslavs, sincerely hoped so.

We had a radio tuned into London and a copy of *The Times* with the constituencies and candidates printed in it. We sat round the radio all day, listening to the returns as they came in. I could not sit, because I had been turned over in a jeep the day before and put my knee out. I remember lying on the floor in front of the radio with *The Times* spread out before me, steadily filling in the results and adding them up. Our excitement grew as the possibility and then the certainty of a majority became clear and, finally, as the size of the majority piled up. We celebrated with Yugoslav sparkling wine and plum brandy. We all believed that a new dawn had broken for the UK, as it had for Yugoslavia.

MICHAEL and ELEANOR BARRATT-BROWN
(Derbyshire Fabians)

✘ When the result was declared we were on a holiday in Southport. We were walking back from the beach one lunchtime when we saw people standing in groups in the middle of the road, talking excitedly. My father rushed into the nearest newsagent's and came out with an early edition proclaiming a Labour victory. My sister and I danced a jig – my mother was in tears – and we were soon all celebrating with complete strangers. This in the middle of Lord Street – the Bond Street of the North!

MARGARET WRIGHT (Suffolk Fabian)

✘ My girlfriend kissed me. That was Stella. We met in the street and she asked what was the result and I said Labour has so many seats and she said 'Oh marvellous' and she threw her arms around me and was so excited. I had never known her to be so excited. She felt heaven had opened at last and now we were going to do something to put the country back on its feet, with all the reconstruction, with all the wonderful ideas. We were going to rebuild society and have fair shares for all, knock down the slums, house all the homeless and convert all our war industries into factories, get rid of the Means Test and build a National Health Service and all the other things.

TOM MELDRUM (Watford Fabian)

✘ I was at Pachmarhi, the hill station, during the hot weather as an instructor at the Army School of Education (India). The General Election at home was followed with the greatest interest by the staff. For one thing, it would probably result, if Labour won, in a different policy for India, even eventual independence. This point was of particular concern for the regular army officers who ruled the school – the commandant and the chief instructor, colonels both – and all those who had served the British Raj for many years. They were natural Conservatives, only at home in the Indian wing of the school where the language was Urdu. They were, however, all at sea in our British wing for there we trained leaders for discussion groups dealing with current affairs in Britain about which they were ignorant. In our wing all the staff were Labour or Liberal supporters or sympathisers. On 26 July, the day on which the election results were announced, there was considerable excitement in our mess. One of us had brought in a blackboard from the lecture room. As the results came through from Delhi Radio, he was busy, jumping up and down during dinner, writing them up on the board while we cheered each victory and the mess servants, in their immaculate white, watched the sahibs with amusement.

PETER KINGSFORD

✘ I was on a troopship going through the Mediterranean on the way to India. Other ranks were packed in like sardines on the troopdecks whereas I shared a two-berth cabin with four others, but did have access to the open boatdeck. When the election results were being broadcast over the ship's public-address system, Labour victories were greeted with resounding cheers from the troopdecks while the faces of the senior officers became longer and longer. 'We'll never win the war now,' was the kind of comment they began to make. Rebellious juniors like myself could only indicate that they could solve their personal problems by jumping overboard if they wanted to.

DAVID PATTERSON

✘ I was working at the gas company. A friend was one of the telephonists there and she rang through to me and said, 'Dotty, Dotty, the results are coming through. It's Labour 99, Conservative 22. I said, 'You must've got it the wrong way round.' She said, 'I haven't,' and the general manager just put his head around the door and said, 'Oh well we'll be nationalised in five minutes.'

DOT VOLLER (Brighton Fabian)

✗ In '45 I was a temporary civil servant. I spent the whole war at the Ministry of Supply mobilising labour for the whole production war effort. Dalton then asked me to come over to the Board of Trade to plan reconversion back to peacetime. We planned the reconversion to peacetime down to every detail, all the major factories, exactly what they would do, and we had agreements with all the major firms so that they could go ahead with these plans without further instruction the moment VE Day was announced. Everyone then feared we would have the frightful post-war slump which occurred 1920–22 after the violent boom in 1920. The plan was to avoid this, which was, in fact, successfully done. I was running this unit under Hugh Dalton and Ernie Bevin as Minister of Labour. We all assumed that the Churchill government would be re-elected and I would have stayed a civil servant.

On the 26 July it was raining very hard, absolutely pelting. I was sitting at my desk at the Board of Trade in the present ICI House and a girl in my department who was extremely efficient put her head around the door and said the Labour Party had won the election. I naturally said, 'You are joking.' The first thing that flashed through my head was the pouring rain, was it going to rain forever like this in peacetime? The second was, Good heavens! All the arrangements we had worked on for fifteen months for industrial turn-round would now not merely be grudgingly and reluctantly accepted by a Tory government but with Dalton as Chancellor and Ernie Bevin in some other senior post, virtually anything I could propose would be pushed through. That was a very exciting moment.

DOUGLAS JAY (MP Battersea. Elected 1946)

CHAPTER SIX

A Funny Thing Happened on the Way to Potsdam

Returning from the first session of Potsdam, Churchill was stunned by first results, which he got while in his bath on 26 July. 'A blessing in disguise,' said Clementine. 'At the moment, it seems quite effectively disguised,' he retorted. It also surprised the Labour leadership. By nightfall Churchill had resigned and Attlee had been asked to form a government. 'Quite an exciting day,' he commented.

✗ We got Mr Attlee to come to a Central London Fabian dance on the night the final election results came out. As I had a car and some petrol left from the allocation they gave us for the election, I and Jack Diamond drove him to his next appointment. He could not stay long at the dance. He seemed very surprised and pleased at the election result, as we all were. We kept saying he must hurry as he had to make a government that night.

PHILIP SOPER

Attlee's task was lonely but hardly difficult. Long service in the wartime Coalition meant that the kernel of Labour leaders had more experience than any incoming government before or since, while the influx of talent gave the Prime Minister a wealth of choice. For the rest of the political nation the more interesting problem was to explain and understand a political revolution which had produced the greatest reversal of the century. Why had a war leader of towering stature been thrown out and Labour brought into power?

✗ Public-opinion polls were very much in their infancy and very amateurish and I don't think there was much indication, even among the people who were supposed to know, that Labour was going to have such a sweeping victory, because Churchill – the Tories – completely misunderstood what was happening, in retrospect. They thought that he would march to victory on the strength of his war record. I think that the Labour Party manifesto was absolutely right when it said that the war had been won, certainly, with a very charismatic leader, but couldn't have been won without the efforts, the great efforts, of ordinary working people, whether it was in the forces or in civilian work, miners and munitions workers, women factory workers. In fact, it was a national effort and it was this national effort that was called for to make sure that we won the peace. We laid down a strategy for winning the peace, socially, economically, politically. It obviously struck a chord in the minds and hearts of millions of folk that wouldn't otherwise have voted Labour and probably haven't voted Labour since.

Lieutenant WILLIE HAMILTON (Labour, West Fife.
Defeated by 2,056 votes by Communist Willie Gallagher)

✗ The pervading sentiment was no return to 1919. After all, it was only twenty years, it was like 1970 as against today, and it was the memory of the ex-servicemen with no legs displaying their medals and playing the cornet on street corners, combined with unemployment in the thirties, that made us all say we are not going back there.

The second important sentiment was that we had convinced ourselves that Beveridge could be applied. I bought a copy of Beveridge and put it in my kitbag in 1943 and carried it with me until the end of the war, and I used to give impromptu talks about it. You can imagine, when people have been at war for three or four years away from their homes and families and not seeing too much of them, all we were interested in was the end of the war and what we were going to do after the war and how soon we could get back into civvy life and get on with things again.

Those were the sentiments; and things like nationalisation, I'm sure they played a large part in some areas, obviously in the valleys where the pits were, and they obviously cared about nationalisation of the pits, but I don't think that was so true of others. Nationalisation was not really an issue. It was more the creation of the welfare state, more the need to demobilise the men and to get Britain working again, all that sort of thing, and the Beveridge Report.

Lieutenant JAMES CALLAGHAN (Labour, Cardiff South.
Majority 5,944)

✗ I personally expected Labour to win and I think most of us in the services did because in a sense we couldn't imagine the electorate voting for the party that had plunged us into the slump in the thirties and had tried to make it up with Hitler. The only real asset the Tories had was Winston Churchill, who was Prime Minister, but he blew it all by the most ridiculous nonsense, like saying that if Labour won Attlee would introduce a Gestapo. I always remember one broadcast in which he talked about, 'You men and women of England, who are listening to me in your cottages.' He really was totally out of touch with the real world and, of course, was always a disaster on domestic policy which is what the election was really about.

I think we won above all because people wanted change. They didn't want to put back the party responsible for the slump and for Munich and I think Labour had won its spurs by its contribution to the war effort in the Coalition government. Bevin was widely and rightly regarded as one of the architects of victory.

Major DENIS HEALEY (Labour, Pudsey and Otley.
Defeated by 1,651 votes)

✗ They had heard about the Beveridge Report, they'd heard about the National Health Service, they'd heard about a full-employment policy and they were absolutely determined that they were going to have those things. They had fought for them, Churchill had not won the war single-handedly, he had required a little help from them, and they were going to get their reward. It was in every sense of the word a civilian war. They'd known that it had been planning and fair shares and strictly fair distributions of the essentials of life that had won the war, and they wanted that in the peace. So they voted for us.

BARBARA CASTLE (Labour, Blackburn.
Second place with 35,145 votes in a two-member borough)

✗ I put it down to the fact that politics had been on ice for five years; there was a great feeling of frustration, of regimentation. Had there been an election when it was due in 1940, I think probably Labour would have won very handsomely. The Tories had been there a long time. Not altogether unlike the current situation.

Lord ANDREW CAVENDISH (Conservative, Chesterfield.
Defeated by 12,035 votes)

✘ At the 1945 election, Common Wealth had about thirty candidates. I had to honour the pledge I'd given at the 1944 by-election, not to fight Labour in Skipton, and stood down then. I'd given it because in 1944, though the real contest was between me and the Conservatives, some of the Labour Party establishment in Skipton were saying that they would support Toole in order to stop me from getting in. They did this because they feared that if I was the sitting MP at the post-war General Election they would find it more difficult to win the seat for Labour. So I gave a public promise not to fight against a Labour candidate at that election, I won the by-election by two hundred votes; without my promise to Labour I would probably have lost. In 1945 therefore I stood at Harrow West, where we had a very strong constituency party. I had a very vigorous campaign but came bottom of the poll behind Conservative, Labour and Liberal. Together with all other Common Wealth candidates, including Acland, I lost my deposit.

HUGH LAWSON (Common Wealth, Harrow West.
Fourth place with 2,462 votes)

✘ I was a gunner, serving with an artillery company in Northern Italy. The mood in the army, certainly in Italy, was a strong indication of left-wing feeling, although we were very short of political news, other than about the Beveridge Report, which had aroused great enthusiasm. It was interesting, in retrospect, to note that the forces' enthusiasm was for 'Labour' – not for 'Socialism' as an abstract conception which seemed to have very little content.

The feeling was very strongly that we could not return to the poverty and unemployment of the thirties, that the differences of social status, which were still maintained by the officers/other ranks split, must be abolished. The sentiment at home that the Tories would probably win was virtually unheard in the regiment as everyone, including the officers who maintained their long allegiance, were quite certain that Labour would win. The ranks thought of any other solution as incredible. Churchill was very unpopular. The troops felt very strongly that 'we' had won the war, and it was an insufferable impertinence for a civilian to claim the credit for what they, the fighting men, had done.

The troops were puzzled by the system of voting, which was not clear to the ordinary soldiers, although I myself think it would have been difficult in the circumstances to have done much better. I got off to a quick start and got my proxy through to my parents who used it. Many men appointed their wives as proxies, but the wives never exercised their votes. In my own regiment the number who voted was almost certainly under a third.

It would have been impossible for anyone, certainly in the ranks, of an active service regiment like ours to have become a candidate. There was some feeling that the system favoured those who were stationed in the UK, or Germany, and had access to the political machinery. We had one bombardier, a Scot, who was a councillor in Leith, who had parliamentary ambitions but found it impossible to get a nomination in the mad scramble of summer 1945. When the results came through there was a general feeling of satisfaction, but no surprise.

JACK GOLDBERG (Manchester Fabian)

✘ The issue that really touched them was the question of Churchill's status in the campaign. The people were grateful to Churchill, but they were disappointed that he was going to fight it as a Conservative. This was the reason. I thought it would go against them. I remember in the middle of the election there was an account of his going up to Nottingham to speak. It was one of these mass rallies where there were six candidates from six constituencies in the Nottingham area and Winston got up, made his big speech, cheers all round the place. He then said, 'I have to go on to another meeting. I commend to you these six candidates.' All the cheers turned to boos. He was committed to supporting people who, everybody knew, had been opposed to him.

There was also, of course, the issue of the Beveridge plan. That was important. The sense that we could achieve full employment. The Beveridge concept was really strong. It was a Liberal idea. We were trying to pick up the goodwill from the Beveridge programme. I expected the Liberals to do better than they did. I didn't expect them to win because they only had three hundred candidates. That was a source of weakness to us; could we form a government? I had really to equivocate to some extent on that one. The business was to get into power, not to play politics, but I couldn't obviously assume that we could get power with only three hundred candidates. So that was in reality a limiting factor for us.

Wing Commander ALAN CAMPBELL-JOHNSON
(Liberal, Salisbury. Third place with 8,946 votes.)

✘ They associated Labour attitudes and policy with a continuation of what they'd become accustomed to during the war. The sharing.

Attlee at Transport House to hear the results

Whether you were rich or poor you were all subject to being bombed out at night. And of course one's speeches accentuated that attitude and the possibility of continuing it after the war. When Churchill came down to Manchester to say his piece, which was a very short piece – namely, 'I've won the war for you, I expect you to vote for me now' – he thought that was adequate. The whole of Manchester turned out to cheer him in the streets and then shortly afterwards to vote Labour in the polling booths. They did not think that the winner of the war was necessarily their leader in peacetime.

JACK DIAMOND (Labour, Manchester, Blackley. Majority 4,814)

✘ On the day of the declaration I went to Transport House. I think we may have had an opinion poll but nobody talked about it and we never thought we would win. Who thought we would beat Churchill? He'd won the war single-handed. So when I was at Transport House, in Transport Hall on the ground floor, we sat there in the dark with the results being written on smoked glass and flashed up on an epidiascope, and the Tory ministers were falling like ninepins. The door opened and there, blinking from the

Central Hall, Westminster, polling-evening meeting

bright sunshine, was Clem, who had just come back from Potsdam and he had been picked up at Northholt by a police car which didn't have a radio. When he arrived he didn't know what had happened and a BBC man came up to me with a microphone and said, 'Will you give three cheers for the Prime Minister.' I was a bit too shy, so somebody else did. But I saw Clem at the very moment when he realised he had become Prime Minister.

That night I went to Central Hall, Westminster, which was packed with Labour supporters. I was up in the gallery looking down and I saw Clem come on to the platform and he said, 'I have just returned from the Palace where the King has asked me to form a government.' The whole place erupted. But what was so exciting about it was that everybody was so surging with confidence. Here we were so utterly bankrupt, saved by the skin of our teeth by the Red Army who carried the brunt of the Nazi attack and then by the Americans who came over and provided the main forces at D-Day, and yet my generation thought we could beat Hitler, beat Mussolini, end the means test, end rearmament, build the welfare state, have the health service. And we did.

TONY BENN

Central Hall, Westminster

✘ The forces' vote was very strong. That's attributed to a great deal of educational work during the war, but educational work can't do all that much unless a mood is running in a certain direction. I think it was the delayed rejection of the Toryism of the 1930s, accompanied by a feeling that the war had been won on a collective basis, and if you could win the war on that basis you could organise the peace on that basis. And also I think that the three or four or five main Labour leaders had become familiar, respected figures who required no great leap of the imagination to see them as being leaders of government. They'd been major figures in the Coalition during the war, and Churchill's rather ill-judged attempt to present them as close colleagues during the war who'd suddenly become wild men overnight, that obviously backfired very heavily.

It wasn't a very high poll but a pretty decisive result. The Labour Party got nearer, I think, than anybody's done since, to winning a majority of those voting. Didn't actually quite do so. It was about 49.9%. But, of course, that's a magnificent performance compared with the 38%, 39% and 40% which great majorities have been elected on since.   Captain ROY JENKINS
(Labour, Solihull. Defeated by 5,049 votes)

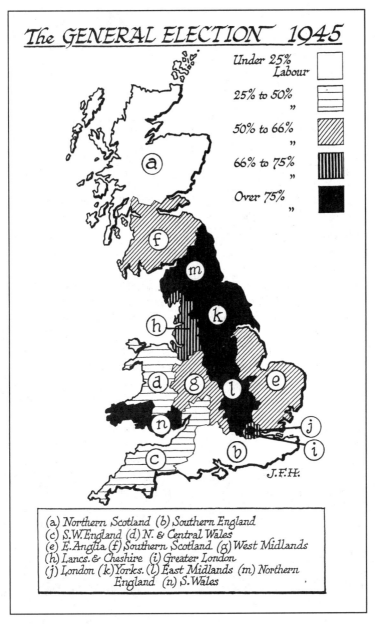

The GENERAL ELECTION 1945

Under 25% Labour

25% to 50% "

50% to 66% "

66% to 75% "

Over 75% "

J.F.H.

(a) Northern Scotland (b) Southern England
(c) S.W.England (d) N. & Central Wales
(e) E.Anglia (f) Southern Scotland. (g) West Midlands
(h) Lancs. & Cheshire (i) Greater London
(j) London (k) Yorks. (l) East Midlands (m) Northern
England (n) S. Wales

From the Fabian Research Series No. 102 by Margaret Cole

CHAPTER SEVEN

We are the Masters Now

Like film characters released from suspended animation as the projector re-starts, the three-week lull was followed by frenzied political activity. Labour took power and its triumphant MPs converged on London to meet at the Beaver Hall on 28 July.

✘ I got to Paddington and stood waiting for a taxi to go to the Beaver Hall. One came along and I jumped in it and said 'Beaver Hall.' I probably told him I was a new Labour Member of Parliament and we were going to go to elect our leader. When we got to the Beaver Hall, he wouldn't take my fare. That was the great mood of the moment. It was a mood of such hope and such aspiration and of something fulfilled. At the meeting I was so ignorant that I didn't understand the undertones and I didn't realise at all there had been this attempted coup against Attlee that was staged by Morrison and others. To me they were all sitting on the platform, a band of brothers united in victory. So I am afraid the possible tensions of the occasion passed over my head, I was just there as one of the rank and file to sit and join in the applause. It went over rather quickly. I don't remember it as a long meeting at all. We elected Clem.

Lieutenant JAMES CALLAGHAN (MP Labour, Cardiff South)

✘ In Beaver Hall members met from everywhere in England. Overwhelming excitement, we all cheered at any excuse. When Attlee arrived and walked on to the platform with Dalton and Bevin, to everyone's amazement he had changed Dalton from being Foreign Minister to Bevin being Foreign Minister overnight. The whisper all around us was that Churchill didn't trust Dalton, but would trust Bevin to do his work as Foreign Minister. Churchill's work. It

was an extraordinary scene because everyone at Beaver Hall heard that story. Dalton was an old Etonian and Churchill thought he could trust Bevin, compared with an Etonian he couldn't trust.

JOHN PLATTS-MILLS (MP Labour, Finsbury)

✘ We had a meeting at the Beaver Hall and on the way down to the meeting I ran into Ellen Wilkinson, who said, 'You won then.' I said, 'Yes.' So she said, 'What seat was that?' I said, 'Chislehurst.' She said, 'My God the revolution has arrived.' The meeting was electric because one of the questions we put was when were we going to get an increase of salary, because a lot of us were out of the forces with no pay. On polling day I had a letter stating, 'If you are elected you may remain in civvy street for the time being. If unelected you are to report at your headquarters by 23.00 hours on the same day.'

The reaction was very sympathetic. The Chancellor said they were considering it, and eventually we got a thousand but a lot of us who were in the forces were released, and lost the bounty that was paid to other forces. So we saw the Minister of Defence and he said I can't help you, I'm in the same boat. We could just about manage on a thousand.

Sergeant GEORGE WALLACE (MP Labour, Chislehurst)

✘ I was very innocent – I didn't know people like Herbert Morrison and company would stand against each other. All the leaders of the Labour Party were more or less saint-like. When we got to Beaver Hall, everybody thought it was awful plain sailing, There was some sort of vague movement going on in the background – Morrison wanted a vote, but that was pretty quickly squashed by Bevin, who wouldn't have any nonsense. He disliked Morrison more than anybody in the world, I think. I rather liked Morrison, he had this wonderful quiff of hair. He complained to me once about why he didn't get the leadership before the war. He said it was all the Freemasons who got together against him, because he was out for a bit and Attlee took over as leader and the Freemasons ganged up against him.

Major WOODROW WYATT (MP Labour, Birmingham, Aston)

The Commons assembled on 1 August. John Parker's wife, Zena, on seeing the new intake, said, 'It looks like an enormous Fabian School.' Churchill's reaction, reported by Woodrow Wyatt, was sourer. 'And they've got all these officers, too?' They met in the House of Lords, the Commons chamber having been destroyed in 1941. On 15 August, the King's Speech announced the new government's radical programme. The Address in Reply debate on the 16th was begun by Major John Freeman, newly elected Labour MP for Watford. The first bill was the Nationalisation of the Bank of England, introduced by Hugh Dalton, as Chancellor of the Exchequer.

✘ We took our seats in the House and I was standing below the Bar with a huge crush. General Mason-Macfarlane, the Labour Member for Paddington, was wheeled in in a wheelchair because he had something wrong with him and we found a space for him; he later became Chairman of the Defence Committee of the Labour Party. There were so many of us who knew so little about things that we spilled over the Bar on to the floor of the House. These big stalwart messengers, all of whom were ex-warrant officers, were physically leaning against us like a football crowd trying to push us back.

Captain Fred Bellenger was standing next to me and I always remember the messenger, leaning and pushing, saying, 'Come on Captain Bellenger you know better than this.' I wondered what he was supposed to know better than that.

Churchill came in with his PPS, Sir George Harvie-Watt, who sat on the bench behind him, and on the second bench also was Colonel Thornton Kemsley, wearing a monocle and army uniform. It was he who struck up with 'For he's a jolly good fellow' to which little Griffiths, I can't remember his Christian name, who was leaning on the Speaker's Chair, a typical miner who had gone through it all and looked as though he had a lot of physical problems, he struck up 'The Red Flag', which we all sang so lustily. Then Clifton Brown, the Speaker, restored order very sensibly by saying in that quiet rather drawling voice he had, 'I wasn't aware that I had been elected to preside over a glee society.'

Lieutenant JAMES CALLAGHAN (MP Labour, Cardiff South)

✘ We weren't demoralised. It made us determined to do what we could to mitigate what we thought would be the harm done by a Socialist government and as soon as Winston appeared that day, when we were all waiting to elect the Speaker, we sang 'For He's a Jolly Good Fellow', and the Labour Party didn't join in. They let us sing it but as soon as we'd sat down from singing it they stood up and sang 'The Red Flag'. They didn't all start off doing that and some of them looked terribly embarrassed. The front bench of the Labour Party, you should have seen their faces when this was done. They realised they'd better not divide the party so they stood up but didn't sing much.

Major DAVID RENTON (MP National Liberal, Huntingdonshire)

✘ Everybody was on top of the world and the idea of being in the same room as people like Clem Attlee and Herbert Morrison and all the rest of them was an experience one only lives through once. It was marvellous. I don't think one was weighed down by the scale of the problems. One knew that there'd been a ghastly mess made with demobilisation after World War I, and that had to be avoided at all costs, but one had such confidence in one's leaders that it was largely a question of elation. You were quite sure that you'd be carried through by this enormous majority and this spirit in the country. The King's Speech was, to me, an extraordinary occasion and it confirmed me in my monarchist leanings, because here was the Crown, the King himself, in person, telling everybody of all the Socialist reforms that the new government was going to put through. They had to accept it, because it came from the monarch's mouth himself. I realised here was the best agency of political revolution that had been invented.

JACK DIAMOND (MP Labour, Blackley)

✗ We all turned up on 16 August, when Jim Griffiths gave his rendering of 'The Red Flag', in which I joined – somewhat hesitantly because I was not fully sure of what the actual words were – and the Speaker told us that it was high time the music ended and that we got on to business. But it was altogether a very nice occasion. John Freeman made a very good speech in the Address that followed the King's Speech. He was extremely good.

I'd only been in the Commons for about a few days, when I was stopped by Nye in the doorway of the Smoking Room. He said, 'Donald, I want you to be my PPS.' I was a bit stunned by that. I accepted it with some considerable awe, because he'd long been a person whom I admired. I wondered why I wasn't exactly popular with the trade union Members of Parliament for some time afterwards, although I eventually got on well with them, because it was a superb cheek to appoint a non-trade unionist, what passed I suppose for a middle-class intellectual. It never occurred to me at that time that the real reason why they were a little off was because I was not a member of a trade union, whereas Nye, being one of the most active trade unionists in South Wales, might have been expected to have appointed a miners' MP to be his PPS.

Major DONALD BRUCE (MP Labour, Portsmouth North)

✗ I remember silly little things like the fact that I came in and I had my lovely new umbrella, a twenty-first birthday present given to me in 1935 but not used for six years, and I hung it up. When I went to fetch it, it had gone. So I thought there was something funny there. That I remember much more than 'The Red Flag', if you want to know.

Brigadier A. R. W. LOW (MP Conservative, Blackpool)

✗ Altogether those first few months were very exhilarating. The Parliamentary Party was very good, brilliant. There were some very, very good people indeed. I liked them all. They were all so different. There were one or two eccentrics. There was a chap there, whose name I've forgotten, a Christian Scientist, who was advocating that Christian Science be put inside the National Health Service. You had your usual nondescripts who spent most of their time down in the Strangers' Bar and didn't bother very much about anything. Some of the mining community, I regret to say. But it was a good party. It was a friendly party, in so far as Ernie Bevin could permit it. Ernie Bevin always tried to isolate what he called the 'bleeding intellectuals' away from the rest, but he didn't generally succeed. There was a good spirit amongst us all, and it wasn't tainted by this overweening personal ambition for jobs or for press coverage. We didn't have that kind of thing. The Commons was more thickly populated then, and as for the Smoking Room, you wouldn't recognise the Smoking Room. Today it's deserted. In those days it was full every day and what happened in the Smoking Room was in fact quite important.

Most of my colleagues were there because they believed in something. The number of real career seekers who wanted to make a living out of it was very, very limited. Most of my friends never thought of promotion. PLP meetings were notoriously ineffective. We'd go along to Room 14. You had various statements about next week's business, then you'd get some observation on policy made by a member who wanted something done in priority over something else. That would last about five minutes, then the trade union MPs would start banging their desks and saying 'vote, vote vote'. Always, if anything started to go a little dodgy for the platform, which it sometimes did, the trade union members stood all around saying 'vote, vote, vote'. They were largely a pushover. There's no doubt about the trade union dominance in those days, or Bevin's control over them for that matter.

Ernie was held to be the big boy. Clem had his own way of doing it. He was an extraordinary person. He spoke very little himself. Clem's way of handling a Parliamentary Party Meeting was very much the same as his attitude in Cabinet. Everybody would say their piece, then Clem said, 'The decision of the Cabinet is . . . ' It was that kind of style. He was always very brief, very much to the point, thanked everybody, assured everybody they were right. He was actually a very good leader of men, not to be underrated at all, and he certainly held the party as a whole in thrall. Everybody knew who was in control.

Major DONALD BRUCE (MP Labour, Portsmouth)

✘ I expected to get a job, yes. You see, I was highly qualified as a KC, and there weren't many in the Labour Party at that time, so I did expect that I would get a job, possibly, if the party won, that I would be Attorney General in the Labour government. I went up to take the Oath of course, among other things, and to see what the place looked like. I was quite new to active politics at that time. I don't think I felt overawed by it at all. I was very interested and amused by it but not overawed. I was a confident young man and it would have been difficult to overawe me in those days. I didn't feel out of place and I was quite welcomed everywhere. No, I was a happy member of the party from that point of view, and of course I knew Attlee, a little. Herbert Morrison I knew well, and I knew various other leaders of the party. So there was no surprise in it from that point of view.

I was detached in the sense that I knew very few people in the party. I'd not been an active member of it for long. I had been a member of the party before the war in a rather minor way, but not active. It was a fairly united party, considering its composition, and, of course, very pleased at becoming victorious. A lot of the members were new and they thought it was their business to be there all the time. Later on, they got to know better.

I thought we were the masters at that time – as undoubtedly we were. But it was an unwise thing to say. If you are the masters in politics it's rather tactless to emphasise the matter too much. You want to exercise the powers of mastership and leadership but not brag about it. It's what you do that matters.

Sir HARTLEY SHAWCROSS (MP Labour, St Helens)

✘ We were regarded as rather worrying by the leadership because there was a left-wing element in the party then. But they kept us under control very simply through the Whips' Office. I don't think any of us realised that the Tories thought the Socialist revolution had begun. I don't think we thought of it like that. We just felt that we had to get things done and we did some rather ambitious things. We settled in on that basis.

I had no influence and I was of no consequence. We were all part of a new crowd that had come in. We were all severely distrusted by the leadership. We were potentially left wing, untutored and so on. I'd just got married and I wasn't a very keen attender at the House. I used to attend every day at first, but then I stopped. The leaders were rather distant. I knew one or two of them and I wasn't ambitious in those days, so I didn't do anything about anything. It was a very easy life. You didn't have to attend because we didn't have very severe whipping, and I used to take my wife to the cinema.

Flight Officer HAROLD LEVER (MP Labour, Manchester Exchange)

MAJOR FREEMAN (WATFORD)

. . . In asking the House to approve this humble Address, I would conclude with one general observation. The country is conscious of the seriousness of the years that lie ahead; but our people are not depressed by the outlook, nor are they overwhelmed by their responsibilities. On the contrary, on every side is a spirit of high adventure, of gay determination, a readiness to experiment, to take reasonable risks, to stake high in this magnificent venture of rebuilding our civilisation, as we have staked high in the winning of the war. His Majesty's Government has been given a clear mandate for decisive action. By its results shall it be judged. I am confident, having heard His Majesty's gracious words yesterday, that His Majesty's advisers are fully equal to their task. We have before us a battle for peace, no less arduous and no less momentous than the battle we have lived through the last six years. Today, we go into action. Today may rightly be regarded as D-Day in the battle of New Britain.

Address in Reply debate, 16 August 1945

✘ Along came John Freeman to move the Address, wearing the uniform of a major in the Rifle Brigade, and poor old Winston was absolutely astonished. I heard him muttering, 'And they've got all these officers, too?' he couldn't believe it. He was a great man, but he always thought of the English people living happily in their cottage homes ready with an open door, and living on – well, I really don't know what. He was much more interested in the great game, the global arrangements and battling with Stalin.

Major WOODROW WYATT (MP Labour, Birmingham, Aston)

✘ I remember John Freeman's moving the Address. He was so handsome. Very upright carriage, curly red hair in those days and a burnished Sam Browne belt and the sun shone down on it from those tall windows and he really looked so distinguished, this young man back from the war.

Then Hugh Dalton came along with the very early bill to nationalise the Bank of England. Old Hugh, a great histrionic character, with insincerity gleaming in those bright blue eyes. He just stood at the Dispatch Box when he got up to move the second reading. He was very tall. Six foot four or five, loomed as you can imagine, over the Dispatch Box. He held up the bill, didn't say anything and just showed it round to everyone. The Tories baying at him. He was just taking advantage of it. We were all thrilled to bits. We all cheered our heads off but I don't think many of us knew too much about the problems that were then besetting the government with the cutting off of Marshall Aid. I don't think it came home to us at the time how serious this would be for us. So we lived probably in an atmosphere of illusion for some time. But even when it became clear we were having all these troubles, enthusiasm was still tremendous.

Lieutenant JAMES CALLAGHAN (MP Labour, Cardiff South)

Now is the time for the new members to come to the aid of the VJ Party.
Kenneth Younger gets to know Grimsby.

CHAPTER EIGHT

Labour's Great Government

The radical programme set out in 'Let Us Face the Future' was enacted and implemented item by item. Yet the nation in which Labour was setting out to build its New Jerusalem was bankrupt, its assets liquidated to fight a war which had accumulated the largest external debt in history. Britain had to pay its way in the world with an economy totally geared to war, its people exhausted, and its world role too heavy to bear.

So Labour's task became to reconcile the ideals and enthusiasms of 1945 with the realities of a sadly diminished Britain. No government could do that on euphoria alone, but Labour added determination, a powerful team of ministers and a majority big enough to do anything. The Tory opposition, initially stunned, revived, reorganised and moved on to the centre ground. Yet though opposition became more effective, Labour's real problem was the underlying weakness of an economy grossly overstretched. The first intimation emerged with the abrupt end of Lend Lease which had kept Britain going.

✘ After about a week of taking my seat in the Commons there happened one of the most important events of all, which I don't think many people other than myself really took much account of. That was the end of Lend Lease. Knowing something of economics and having studied the position of the country *vis à vis* the world, this caught me in the belly, and, looking back on it, it was from that day, only five days after being returned to Westminster, we were put on the defensive. We knew the economic problems that were already stored up – and damn it all, we'd suffered at 1945 prices some £8 billion worth of damage and loss, one way or another, due to the war. That put us all on the defensive and it made me very apprehensive. Thereafter, my life in politics tended always to be tinged with anxiety. So, rather than going there triumphant, which many of my colleagues were, from the beginning I had this fear that, owing to this very sudden and, indeed, unwarranted cessation of Lend Lease, we were going to be hard put to it doing what we'd said we were going to do.

I had faith, of course, in Keynes, because whatever anybody else said in the party, it was really Keynesian politics that everyone was really aiming at at the time – more especially after the Coalition white paper of 1944 on employment (which, if I may say so, is far more progressive than the policies of the party today). However, we battled on.

Major DONALD BRUCE (MP Labour, Portsmouth South)

✖ The first bit of nationalisation was the Bank of England which didn't take long and was a very short bill. Then the next bit of controversial legislation, which split all the parties, was the government's proposal to raise a loan of a thousand million pounds from the United States. Multiply by fifteen and in modern terms that's fifteen billion pounds, which is a huge loan. A number of Labour members joined with us in voting against it; I think exactly one hundred of us from all parties voted against our raising that loan. We thought we ought to pull ourselves up by our own bootstraps; and it was a shambles because when the money was paid instead of it being used to regenerate British industry it was found that it had to be used to pay off debts still owing to the Egyptians of all people, and in India and elsewhere, debts owing because of the expenses incurred in maintaining the British army in those countries. So this loan which won't be repaid fully until I think the year AD 2000 really was of very little benefit to our country.

Major DAVID RENTON (MP National Liberal, Huntingdonshire)

✖ Divisions appeared, first of all led by me, I'm sorry to say, over demobilisation. Mason-Macfarlane, our general, although he was Chairman of the Defence Committee, didn't really play any part. I had been elected Secretary. I was arrogant even in those very earliest days to get myself elected Secretary. I was really conscious about this demob thing so I pressed very strongly for demobilisation.

Alexander was the Secretary of State for Defence and the service estimates were coming up in February 1946 and he knew that I was going to make a lot of trouble at the estimates. So he came to me just before Christmas 1945 and said, 'We have had an invitation

Britain's Labour government

from the Soviet government, from Mr Stalin personally, asking for a group of young people who served in the war and would care to go to Russia, as they would like to show them some of the things that have happened. Will you go?' He said, 'If you go, you put on your uniform again and you'll get your service pay and, what's more, you'll get hard-living money because Russia is a very difficult station.' Well who could resist that? So I'm afraid I left demobilisation and went off to Russia for six or seven weeks. It was an experience I shall not forget. It always made me feel very warm towards the Russians.

When I came back poor George Isaacs was in charge of the Ministry of Labour, as we called it then, and I got a reduction in the period of conscription and hastened demobilisation. Divisions appeared then. It was mostly servicemen against the rest. Then divisions appeared over steel and over the economic situation. In those days we sat not only on the government side, we sat on the opposition side too, all the way up those lower benches there. I used to sit on the other side, not because I felt opposed, but I used to sit on that side where roughly the Liberals now sit. We stretched all the way up there. Quite extraordinary.

Lieutenant JAMES CALLAGHAN (MP Labour, Cardiff South)

✘ The reputation of the Fabian Society was very high indeed. Every time the 1945 government introduced a new nationalisation measure they said to the House, 'It's all right, you needn't be worried about this. It's all been examined by the Fabian Society and they've made a report in its favour.' This went for pretty well all these outrageous nationalisation proposals that we were putting through. That was the knowledge people, who weren't members of the Fabian Society, had of the society. It was a society which had, before 1945, examined everything that ought to be done, told us how it should be done, reported in favour of these truly Socialist measures, and Bob's your uncle! There was no need to propagate in favour of the Fabian Society. The Fabian Society was the research body of the Labour Party.

JACK DIAMOND (MP Labour, Blackley)

✘ I was depressed but I thought, well, if that's the mood of the country we have got to fight back, haven't we. We were shocked to begin with and obviously Winston was shocked. It was October, November before we began to conspire and consult, get together and begin moving. We were all pretty tired. I was whacked, after four years' fighting. I left Liverpool in a convoy at the end of October 1940 and I got back by aeroplane on the 24 May 1945 and that's a long time. I hadn't been home. So you didn't need me to persuade you that people were tired, and obviously Winston was very tired and there were other things on his mind.

We licked our chops a bit and waited to see how we pulled together and we took the Eden and Rab Butler leadership, particularly the younger ones of us who liked those two and liked what they stood for. We watched them make their speeches and I did two books of speeches for Anthony Eden and I got very keen on the way we were moving towards the type of Conservatism I wanted in 1939.

Brigadier A. R. W. LOW (MP Conservative, Blackpool)

✘ I can't tell you how one was affected by the legislation which was being introduced by that first Labour government. Everything one had aspired to, lo and behold, there were these giants of men. A Chancellor of the Exchequer, who was expected to be as hard as flint, standing up at the Dispatch Box and proposing all sorts of ways in which the public money should be spent for the benefit of the whole of society. It was just marvellous. And nationalisation, one believed in nationalisation at that point.

The odds were that you had perhaps two chances a year to make a real speech. During the course of one of my speeches I just happened to say, perhaps a little naïvely but I certainly said it sincerely, 'Well of course, nobody believes in Clause IV any longer.' This was about 1947 or '48, and the only interruption I got was from a famous Communist member sitting in the House at that time, who said something like, 'Listen to this company director telling us about Clause IV.' From a seated position. But there was hardly a ripple among the rest.

JACK DIAMOND (MP Labour, Blackley)

✘ We had a thing called 'Keep Left' and we wrote a pamphlet and I had a bit about demobilisation written and said it ought to be happening much faster. Attlee got very cross at one party meeting and said there was I, a major, who ought to know better than to say things like that. I don't quite know why he said it, because it was true. You could have got them home a bit quicker. In India, when I went back on a parliamentary delegation in the winter of 1945, there was a mutiny among the RAF. They were in a terrible state; Strachey, who was at the War Office I think, sent me a message, would I go down to see what I could do. So I addressed all the mutineers; they were pretty bloody annoyed. I stood on the platform and then I shut up for a bit and I told them some crap about the *Queen Elizabeth* going back and forth every day and it would take ages to get them all out and to calm down. Well, they didn't like the food or the pay, they were fed up. But I had put down a mutiny. It was quite amusing.

There were faults in the arrangement that we were hanging about a bit. There was a shortage of ships but it always sorted itself out. I agreed with everything in that pamphlet at the time because as far as I can remember every single thing in it was done, so really it wasn't such a revolutionary affair. The only thing we didn't do was build ourselves up as a great bridge between Russia and America. Rather an impractical thought.

Major WOODROW WYATT (MP Labour, Birmingham, Aston)

✘ On Thursdays we always had Herbert Morrison versus Churchill. It got into a personal campaign. It was called Business of the House but on one occasion Churchill, who suffered with blood pressure, seized the books from the table, threw them over the floor and muttered across, 'I'll break your bloody neck for you,' to

Morrison and stamped out. The Speaker didn't hear that. But Edith Summerskill who was sitting near me, said 'I must go out. The old man's got blood pressure. I'm looking after him.' And she went out and looked after him. Actually, she did unofficial medical advice for Winston.

Sergeant GEORGE WALLACE (MP Labour, Chislehurst)

✖ I had the good luck of being a coalminer and I was welcomed by the lads as a genuine coalminer, which I wasn't at all, of course. I was from the far end of the world and spoke southern English as compared to a coalminer. But they took me on board like anything. I was asked to propose the health of the Cabinet at the first miners' dinner given to the Cabinet. I thought that was rather good.

Everyone turned up. All the time. There was no let up until Christmas. Everyone stayed. I was unconscious of a whip until the third year. I missed pretty well every first vote. I got there for Question Time when I got back from chambers. I'm sure coming from the North of England that was too bad, but every Londoner was back at work. The pay wasn't enough really for a middle-class chap. There was a great feeling that went on for quite a while. Even the summer and the strawberries on the terrace added to the magic. Everything about the place was magic. No one could be better looked after than by the servants of the House.

We had to carry out a revolution but I think our leaders were determined there wasn't to be a revolution. Later on, but not for us. We thought that we would make enormous changes, we would nationalise everything. And we got a good beginning. I was proud to be a part of that.

JOHN PLATTS-MILLS (MP Labour, Finsbury)

✖ The PLP was really full of hope and glory. We were on a crusade, a great mission. It was regarded as a vocation almost and the general thrust of loyalty, pride and success carried one a long way into '47, '48, '49.

The only jarring note was Dick Crossman. Dick had moved a famous amendment to the debate on the Address in 1946 which said Bevin ought to do everything Mr Molotov told him to. At the conference in 1947 there was Ernie, the real power and strength of the Labour government as Foreign Secretary, but he was not a member of the NEC. So, by the rules of the party, he had to walk down to the lower-level rostrum and speak for five minutes.

However, he rolled up to the top level and talked for sixty-five minutes about how in '46 he travelled to Washington in order to persuade the Americans to direct ships carrying a hundred thousand tons of wheat from the US to here, to India instead, to avoid total and immediate starvation. At the height of this dramatic story he paused and lowered his voice to a whisper which was heard by over three thousand people. 'That was the moment they chose to stab me in the back.' The whole audience roared – the largest applause I've ever heard.

DOUGLAS JAY (MP Labour, Battersea. Elected in 1946)

✘ Ernie Bevin was stabbed in the back by Dick Crossman. I'm afraid I was one of the signatories to that thing. I felt rather ashamed of myself later as I got to know Ernie after a bit. He was very upset. Said I didn't understand anything about foreign policy at all – he was right of course.

Major WOODROW WYATT (MP Labour, Birmingham, Aston)

✘ There was a mood of building and don't let's have it wrecked by discontented people who thought they should have been promoted. There is always one third of the PLP who are slightly unreliable, but the two thirds were solid and attendance was large. We were exceedingly conscientious and took things seriously. If Clem or Morrison got up and said, 'Look here, what you're suggesting isn't practical and would cause great trouble,' it went down well, and was always accepted. That was how it all was after the war; and we introduced the NHS, national insurance, public ownership of the coal industry, which all went through in eighteen months.

It was a very successful government. We demobilised in record time, much faster than after World War I, and avoided the unemployment that followed that war. In fact, unemployment never rose above three per cent in the whole of that government. We saw that financially and economically we were in a state of absolute collapse. The current rate at which we were losing gold would have left us, by December '45, entirely unable to buy food from the US, and the ration would not merely have gone down to half of wartime but to nothing. Meanwhile the whole country thought the war was over and everything should now improve. First we negotiated the American loan, which kept going until '47, then the convertibility clause swallowed all that up. Then Marshall

Chancellor Dalton and Evan Durbin

Aid saved everything. That carried us through.

Economic policy was in chaos in 1945–7, which Harold Wilson repeated from 1964 to '66. People looked to a sort of ideal economic future which bore no relation to what our actual resources were. Economics to Dalton, as to all pre-1930s English economists, was the study of the British economy, not all that stuff about the exchange rate. Balance of payments in the 1920s and '30s was one annual article in the *Board of Trade Journal* by a boy called Bailey. He put forth some figures and people politely noticed them. Dalton had been brought up on public finance, to think of tax-enriched financing of the social services, and regenerating the old depressed areas. When you told him you needed dollars he didn't understand. That sort of thing was understood by Balogh and Kaldor, those funny men whom he called Buda and Pest, which didn't create much goodwill in Whitehall. It was sheer muddle. Morrison was in economic control but didn't understand the economic processes. He had the lawyer's approach.

It all completely changed because we brought all these people into the Treasury who had been colleagues of mine in the war effort, all first-class people. Stafford Cripps was marvellous because, although he did not have the natural instinctive understanding of the economic process which Ernie had to the fingertips, when he got the hang of the thing he would stick to it and put it through, having decided it was God's will. So we then had this powerful triumvirate, with the unbreakable link between Attlee and Bevin, two totally separate men who totally trusted each other. Edward Bridges was the Secretary to the Cabinet, Head of the Civil Service, a man with enormous prestige whose job was to prevent chaos and muddle. Knowing that Stafford and all these modern economic advisers and Keynesians were pushing their way of doing things, his job wasn't to criticise it but to see that it bloody well went through, and it did in a record of success which no government has equalled.

DOUGLAS JAY (MP Labour, Battersea. Elected 1946)

CHAPTER NINE

1945 and All That

'You've had a revolution,' said President Truman to George VI. 'Oh no,' said the King, 'we don't have those here.' R. B. McCullum and Alison Readman make the same point in the first Nuffield election study. Revolution is a justifiable expression but one it might be well to avoid. This was British and democratic, but 'in its true political sense, a revolution is an especially forcible substitution by subjects of a new ruler or policy for old'.

In the light of the subsequent difficulties of securing change in Britain's conservative body politic, we can omit 'forcible' and see 1945 as the nearest thing to a revolution we British are likely to get: an electoral overthrow, opening the way to a massive programme of change and shaping a new settlement which endured for more than three decades. The underdogs bit back.

> Grim was it in that dawn to be alive,
> Except to those who like their mornings bloody.
> The ship of state headlong was seen to dive,
> Engulfed in depths unutterably muddy.
> As Jacobins, like swarms that leave the hive,
> Belched forth from foundry, factory and study,
> A cut-throat crew of howling demagogues,
> Leading hereditary underdogs.
>
> 'Let Cowards Flinch' by Sagittarius

Conservatives saw it as a drastic shock and coped in Whig fashion by absorption rather than resistance, moving to the centre ground to administer the new settlement rather than reverse it. Socialists saw *it as a new dawn of a new world. The impetus might run down —*

> *In Britain reckless progress is arrested,*
> *Her constitution jibs at changes drastic,*
> *Newfangled propositions are digested*
> *By processes not cerebral but gastric.*
> *But once experiments are tried and tested*
> *Her system is prodigiously elastic . . .*

but only because revolution had become part of the status quo. Like Labour.

Later revisionists, such as Paul Addison in The Road to 1945, *made the obvious point that Labour was less about socialism than continuity; a prolongation of the wartime state power, collective effort, controls, intervention and common concern. That is clearly true, but minimising neither the contrast with pre-war norms, nor the importance of dedicating peacetime society to the common man by running it for jobs, growth and welfare.*

So the real change in attitudes towards 1945 was rejection as Britain's comparative economic failure generated alienation from the 1945 settlement making it an object of blame rather than praise. As they became more ideological, Conservatives launched a counter revolution, to turn both levers of power and the clock-hands back, against the 1945 settlement. Corelli Barnett argued that the British people were rewarded too well after the war, making them too comfortable, too prone to consume, to compete in a world growing harder and colder. Thatcherism revived a Hewart/Hayek tradition eclipsed in 1945 and hostile to public ownership and spending, to equality, state power and welfare. After 1979 all were rolled back as the Tory Party dedicated itself to undoing 1945.

Labour's response was bemused for 1945 had petrified into myth, its achievements into orthodoxy, creating a complacent feeling that we were and would remain the masters. 1945 had made Labour a majority party, the natural party of government and, so David Butler and Donald Stokes told us in the sixties, the natural majority party. The consequence was stultification.

For the left the myth of 1945 was that strong principles, firmly proclaimed, would evoke a latent radicalism in British breasts. The Labour right saw it as a final settlement, to be administered but not substantially changed. Neither updated its thinking or adjusted structures becoming arthritic to the new consumer society. Both treated the shrinking working class like Pavlov's dogs rather than as consumers to be persuaded. Intellectual debate became a game of pat ball, juxtaposing a simplistic Crossman/Benn 'stick to our principles' stereotype against a Crosland/Blair 'kill sacred cows' argument while social change, electronic politics and economic failure made the whole debate irrelevant, undermining the base of the 1945 settlement and of the party itself. So revolution ended as rear-guard action. The 1974–9 Labour government struggled to defend the 1945 settlement and keep its rickety structures functioning.

What began with a bang ended as a prolonged whimper and electoral rejection. The strain of clinging to the wreckage by incomes policy and expenditures financed out of taxation broke the Labour movement. 1945's praetorian guard, the skilled workers, began to desert. Union militants vandalised its structures. Ideologues denounced its heirs as traitors. Labour was thrown from power as a result. Bringing the end of the generation, the attitudes, the structures, and the world of 1945. The Tories moved in as demolition gang.

Labour watched the vandalism with gulping incredulity for the trauma of rejection had brought on a collective nervous breakdown reducing the party to a nadir comparable only to 1931. Yet 1945 came a mere fourteen years after 1931 and now, a similar period after 1983, a recovered and revived party wonders if it is seeing the development of a similar seismic shift to jolt the nation on to a new course. Hope springs eternal. Fortunately so for a party which has spent thirty-two years of the half-century since it began to reshape the world, in opposition. Yet discounting surging hopes, the 1945 victory was built on:

FIRST   *The weakening and inattention of the forces of conservatism, which had been so strong for so long; the Tory majority and its machine; the Conservative hegemony in the media; systemic inertia; and the electorate's fear of change.*

SECOND   *Massive alienation from the incumbent Conservative government, built up by its failures and incompetence but heightened by an overwhelming feeling of 'time for a change'.*

THIRD   *The offer of an alternative world, relevant to the real needs of the people, defensible in terms of their own experience and energetically propagated.*

FOURTH   *The rise of a new majority, taking power to reshape and run society in its favour.*

FIFTH   *Governments lose, oppositions don't win, but they can smooth the process by experience, attractiveness and relevance, as Labour, in government since 1940, did in 1945.*

Brought together in the pressure-cooker of war these ingredients produced 1945, a conjunction which can't be repeated. Today the pressure cooker is switched off. The world had changed. The testing and projection of leadership is done by the media, not real experience in government. The working class was the broad base of the pyramid but now society swells out towards the middle with those lower down, an alienated sub-class. Voicing the views of 'the people' is more difficult in a pluralistic, individualised society. Politics is no longer a crusade but a consumer sales pitch as customers look for the best buys, the media become the middlemen and leaders imitate salespeople whose pitch is as important as their programme.

In such a bizarre new world hoping for a repetition of 1945 is a distracting dream. Yet enough of the ingredients of the victory are now back in place to make major change possible. The first and second factors are present. Indeed the electorate's desire for a new beginning runs ahead of Labour's cautious offerings because the party still lacks confidence, anxiously trying to make amends for its own follies, rather than developing a firm, confident programme for power, such as it had in 1945.

Thus the challenge becomes one of using the last months of opposition to add the third element, so that Labour does not come to power without an idea in its head about how to use it and what to do. Such a disaster can be avoided only by developing plans and programmes to fulfil the expectations which will take Labour to power, so that in government it shifts balances to fairness, security, community – management rather than markets and public rather than private. That is what the mass of the people wants and it demands going back to the basics of 1945: full employment, economic growth, universal healthcare, and the best education and welfare to make the world right for the majority, whether called the multitude who labour, the working class or simply 'the people'.

Of the five degrees on the 1945 Richter Scale, Labour is already at 2 but needs 2.79 to 3. The first priority must be to reach that level quickly. Opportunities for change are rare in Britain because Labour always runs the electoral race with a ball and chain. So as opportunity opens up and the shackles are eased Labour must seize its moment with the enthusiasm and steady hand it had in 1945, with simple bold policies and clear-headed determination to use power to build anew. The real message of 1945 lies neither in its legend and the attendant myths, nor in any attempt to get back to its by re-organising the rubble. What 1945 shows is just what is possible when a party with firm priorities seizes its moment to address the real and present problems of the people. Some veterans of 1945 feel that the opportunity is now returning. At long last.

✘ In some regards I think we are back to 1945. There is an atmosphere, you can sense it when you walk about amongst the ordinary people. I have no official position today, I've got far too old. But I do meet a lot of people and there is the sort of reaction I got in 1945. In 1945 what you heard everywhere was, 'Churchill was a good leader in war, but he is no good for peace'; today people are saying, 'Major and his government are no good for the present age in which we live, and it's time we had a change, and a change can only be a Labour Party – a Labour government.' This is what I find amongst ordinary folk. This is not anything that I receive from any official quarters. It's just one's sense. And I've been in the political realm for too many years to be hoodwinked. This is a genuine feeling like the genuine feeling that was apparent in that first election that I fought fifty years ago.

BERT HAZELL (Labour, Barkston Ash)

List of those interviewed

Lord Aldington
Tony Benn
Lord Bottomley of
   Middlesbrough
Lord Bruce of Donington
Lord Callaghan of Cardiff
Alan Campbell-Johnson
Leonard Caplan QC
Baroness Castle of Blackburn
Frank Clayton
Lord Cledwyn of Penrhos
Lord Diamond
The Duke of Devonshire
Marjorie Durbin
Dorothy Fox
Willie Hamilton
Lord Harmar-Nicholls of
   Peterborough
Bert Hazell
Lord Healey of Riddlesden
Lord Jay

Lord Jenkins of Hillhead
Sir John Junor
Dr Peter Kingsford
Lord Lever of Manchester
F. Ashe Lincoln QC
Laddie Lucas
Stella and Tom Meldrum
Philip Owen
John Platts-Mills
Lord Renton of Huntingdon
Lord Shawcross of Friston
William Shepherd
Dot Voller
Irene Wagner
Lord Wallace of Coslany
Archie Waters
Baroness White of Rhymney
Lord Wigoder of Cheetham
Sir Paul Wright
Lord Wyatt of Weeford.

Those who contributed recollections and material

Lord Amery of Lustleigh
Kenneth Baker MP
Professor Stuart Ball
Michael and Eleanor Barratt-
   Brown
Rt Revd Stanley Booth-
   Clibborn
Roderic Bowen
Christopher Boyd

Lord Boyd-Carpenter of Crux
   Easton
Hans Breitenbach
L. W. Clarke
Hugh Cockerell
Horace Trevor Cox
William Crawley
Simon Wingfield Digby
Peter Dimoldenberg

Viscount Eccles
Arthur Edwards
Viscount Esher
Gwynfor Evans
Ewan Faulkner
Lord Glendevon
Maria and Jack Goldberg
Llin Golding MP
Stella Greenall
Wing Commander Sir Robert
   Grant-Ferris
Lord Harvington of Nantwich
Beryl Hughes
Walter James
Aubrey Jones
David Jones
Viscount Lambton
Hugh Lawson
Sir Edwin Leather
Geoffrey D. Lewis

Sir Kenneth Lewis
Sir Fitzroy Maclean
Ron Major
Dr David Patterson
R. S. Pease
Susan Pomeroy
Professor Peter Pulzer
Peter Self
Dr Konrad Singer
Philip Soper
Sir Rupert Speir
Shaun Stewart
Harold Taylor
Peter Trench
Henry Usborne
Jack Vincent
David Williams
Margaret Wright
Christopher York
Sam Younger.

Illustrations

British Library; Centre for the Study of Cartoons and Caricature, University of Kent, Canterbury; *Daily Express*; *Grimsby Evening Telegraph*; Hulton Deustch Collection; Museum of Labour History; Fabian Society: Marjorie Durbin, Dr Peter Kingsford, Professor Peter Pulzer, Baroness White, Bert Hazell.